ONE HONEST MAN

FOUR DIFFERENT PERSPECTIVES.

FORTY-FIVE YEARS AS AN **AYR UNITED FAN**

ONE HONEST MAN

FOUR DIFFERENT PERSPECTIVES.

FORTY-FIVE YEARS AS AN **AYR UNITED FAN**

First published in Great Britain in 2012 by The Derby Books Publishing Company Limited, 3 The Parker Centre, Derby, DE21 4SZ.

ISBN 9781780910703

Printed and bound by Gomer Press, Llandysul Ceredigion.

Contents

Introduction

For many people brought up in Scotland, the national sport has played a big part in their lives. For me it is no different. I have been involved in the game in a variety of roles and that has given me the benefit of seeing football from four different perspectives. I am hoping that in writing this book I can share my observations and experiences with people who perhaps have only had the benefit of seeing the game from one, two or three of these angles. What I mean is, I can think like a player, a coach, a fan and a referee. Developing my experience in the game from all of these angles has proved to be an interesting and rewarding pastime and I am hopeful that the readers of this book can relate to my story.

The famous poet Robert Burns referred to my home town in his epic poem *Tam o' Shanter* and the local football team adopted, as a nickname, his description of the male inhabitants of the town.

Auld Ayr, wham ne'er a town surpasses
For honest men and bonnie lasses

In my time in football I have experienced the highs and lows of my favourites and I am proud to say that I am an 'Honest Man'. I was born in Peebles Street, Ayr in 1954 and I have had a lifelong obsession with my beloved Ayr United. From my first match as a 12-year-old in February 1967 to the present day I have endured the insults, derogatory comments and the condescending remarks that go with supporting my wee team but I would not have it any other way. I have memories to share of following Ayr United in matches at Somerset Park and in games all over Scotland and into England.

My second perspective as an 'Honest Man' comes from the angle of a football player. At a very young age I had a fascination for football that has never diminished over the years. I learned my basic skills on a small grassed area at the foot of Dunlop Terrace in Hayhill, along with the large number of kids who occupied the council houses at the bottom of the Craigie housing estate. Like any other group of children at the time, we played football all evening until dark and we only stopped when we could not see the ball anymore. Our weekends gave us the chance to play 'big' games of 15-a-side or more. Ah, happy days. As a growing lad I played school and youth club football before eventually moving on to play in amateur and pub league teams as a young man. I have plenty of anecdotal evidence of the ups and downs of a failed football player that can be described as funny, sad and at times scary.

My perception as a coach, manager and chairman of a local youth club and also an amateur team over a 14-year period has given me another angle on football altogether. My third assumed role as an 'Honest Man' gave me an experience that has opened my eyes to the ruthless nature of people involved in football at the grass roots. It has also provided me with interesting and enjoyable recollections of incidents and has allowed me to meet an array of characters well worth their place in my story. Hilarious, disappointing and outrageous events have provided me with tales that many people in minor grade football will be able to relate to.

My fourth standpoint as an 'Honest Man' was developed from my role as a referee and while some people regard match officials with disdain, I look back on my four-year stint as a referee as a very rewarding and satisfying experience. Refereeing completed a circle for me. Until recently, I was working with missing information and I now have a more holistic view of the game thanks to officiating in matches I previously only attended as a fan, player, coach, manager or committee member. The last four years have filled in the gaps for me. I now have a wider understanding of the game. I want to add my opinion from the viewpoint of a referee to inform people and to explain what it is like on the other side of the touchline.

An Honest Man For Life

My experience of supporting Ayr United has been a roller-coaster ride of emotions and although the cleaners in the Somerset Park boardroom have never needed to overspend their budget on silver polish, that fact has yet to dampen my enthusiasm for following my home town team since 1967.

My family's association with the club was established a long time before I was born. My grandfather, Antonio Mancini, rented the kiosks at Somerset Park and my mother was responsible for the one in the main stand when she was in her early twenties. In 1939, my Uncle Ralph, the youngest of the Mancini family at the age of eight, had his eye on a special job at home games and eventually he persuaded his dad to let him join the ranks of the 'Chocolate Boys'. These were a group of youngsters who carried trays of chocolate round the track at half-time, selling to the crowd and earning pocket money for themselves. My uncle described to me how he earned a penny for every shilling he collected. On his first day in the job he was paid a grand total of nothing. He explained that when he returned to the pavilion and counted his takings, he had somehow lost a shilling and that was precisely what he would have earned from his work on the day. It was an expensive lesson to learn.

My own introduction to football, in an indirect way, was on the day of my birth, 8 December 1954. The doctor had been called to the family house in Peebles Street in Ayr as my mother's fifth child was about to arrive. Doctor McCarroll pulled up outside the house and a group of his friends remained in the car as he dealt with the small matter of delivering me into the world. Apparently, the horn on the car was being sounded regularly to communicate to the physician that time was running out. The group of friends were anxious about getting to Glasgow for the international match and I was an inconvenience to them. As soon as the doctor had carried out his duty, he raced out to the car and off they sped to join 113,000 spectators at Hampden Park. On a bitterly cold day, they watched Scotland lose 4-2 to Hungary.

I was obsessed with football in my early years and I rarely spent time without a ball at my feet. I was introduced to the terraces at the ripe old age of 12. I can clearly remember walking down Craigie Road in Ayr with my brother Tony who, on the way, was engrossed in conversation with a dark haired man. I had no idea who this guy could be but the chat between my brother and the man soon enlightened me. Tony seemed very excited about their discussion and he was firing all sorts of questions at the stranger, about the match and how he thought it would go, as if he would know more than the next person. As it turned out, he did know more than most. The stranger was none other than Peter Price, the retired Ayr United striker. My brother's parting comment to the man was, 'Great to speak to you Peter, good luck.' He then spent the next 10 minutes telling me how lucky I was to be speaking to an Ayr United legend. The fact that I never uttered a word and the legend never once looked at me was lost on my brother who was obviously feeling a deep affinity with his hero. So, I never did get to see Peter Price play for the club and apparently I missed out big time. Nevertheless, that first game provided me with enough excitement to ensure that I was completely hooked. It was a 3-3 draw with Motherwell on a cold Saturday afternoon in February 1967 that lit a fire in me that will never be extinguished. The fact that Ayr were relegated that season was totally lost on me and my affinity with Ayr United has never wavered from that day to this. So, while my friends opted for one or other of the Old Firm to follow, I stuck with the 'Honest Men'. At that time, nobody

I knew actually went to Glasgow to watch their team but I was a regular visitor to Somerset Park and I felt that the club belonged to me. From that day to this, there have been many more disappointments than triumphs but my decision to make Ayr United my team is one I have never regretted. Over the years I endured a barrage of insults and condescending remarks from schoolmates whose allegiance was primarily to Celtic but I learned to live with it. I went to a Roman Catholic secondary school, Queen Margaret Academy, having articulated from St Catherine's Primary School in Dalmilling in 1966. I loved every day at St Catherine's. My teachers were all great and I seemed to be a favourite with a few of them. My final two years there were very eventful. In primary six, I managed to break into the school football team and in primary seven I was picked regularly. Playing football was everything to me and I could not wait for the weekend. My excitement was magnified one Tuesday when our teacher announced that we would be playing a game against Heathfield Primary on the Wednesday and the players chosen for the team would be allowed to leave early to go to the match at the Oval in Prestwick. The team, as usual, was pinned up on the notice board in the corridor outside our class and at lunchtime on the Tuesday a crowd gathered to check out who had been picked and in what position. Big Peter McColm, who would undoubtedly be playing at centre-half, was obscuring my line of sight, preventing me from seeing the team. Once he had surveyed the selections, he turned around and as he passed me he said, 'It's awright Ferrara, don't worry, you're in the team'. Although this brought a smile to my face, I had to see for myself. When I finally managed to worm my way to the front I discovered that I was on the left wing. I was not too chuffed about that as I was definitely an inside-right and outside-left certainly did not appeal. I was in the team though and that was the main thing. I would not be jeopardising my position in the team by complaining about my position in the team, if you get my meaning. The following day dragged but as the afternoon class started my excitement and anticipation grew. I was in a bit of an agitated state and when Mr McVey, our teacher and football team manager, told me off for talking in class for the second time I foolishly never heeded the warning and it was third time unlucky for me. 'Ferrara, out front, now,' I was up on my feet and out at the front of the class in double quick time. I did not want to annoy him more than I had already. Mr McVey was six foot tall, dark haired and always dressed in a smart suit. He had some sort of disability that necessitated a heavy limp when he walked. He was always perfectly nice to me but I was quite scared of him. 'Your disobedience will now be punished,' he said in a very formal voice. 'You have two choices. Either you miss the match and stay in class…' My heart skipped a beat; I was filled with dread. '…or you take three of the belt. What's it to be?' Phew! I had been worried for a second. The relief that the alternative punishment brought was immediate. I never replied, I just raised my hands and straightened my arms out in front of me in the traditional way, palms up, left hand on top of right and awaited my fate. There was no decision to make. There was no way I was forfeiting my place in the team. Mr McVey slipped his right hand under his jacket and pulled out the two-tongued leather strap, which had been strategically placed over his shoulder and under his jacket. After three whacks on alternate palms, my hands stung and I had to work hard to hold back a tear. It was worth it for both of us. He had managed to shut me up for the rest of the class and I still had my place in the team. Everyone wins. I played on the left wing, kitted out in the school colours, white with a large red 'V' on front, apparently donated by Airdrie Football Club because our head teacher once played for them. The game itself was an anticlimax. I rarely saw the ball in a one-sided 3-0 defeat.

My transition from primary to secondary school was fairly smooth but secondary education was something I didn't enjoy one bit. My cohort were the initial, first year group in the newly built Queen Margaret Academy, so everyone was new, not just the first year pupils. The school campus was directly adjacent to the brand new Mainholm Academy. The two secondary schools, one Protestant and one Catholic, sat side by side on Mainholm Road. I do not know which bright spark planned that but it was a recipe for trouble. Bigotry was rife at the time and every few days the word would spread around the playground that there was going to be a big battle at lunchtime outside the school gates. The 'Proddies' were coming over to sort out the 'Papes' or the 'Fenians' were going next door to teach the 'Orangemen' a lesson. It made for good viewing and as long as I kept a careful distance I got to enjoy the gratuitous violence without any of the associated pain. Having the new school built there was very handy for me, my four brothers and two sisters as we lived in Dunlop Terrace in Hayhill which was a 10 minute walk away at the bottom end of Ayr Racecourse. In my Queen Margaret years, Catholics supported Celtic and the idea of supporting Rangers was considered ludicrous. For some people it still is.

Although I was roundly ridiculed for supporting Ayr United, my opinion is that many of my peers missed out on so much over the years. The only time they saw their team was an occasional look at the highlights of Rangers or Celtic matches on BBC's *Sportscene* on a Saturday night or *Scotsport* on STV on a Sunday afternoon. Live matches on television were a rarity.

Watching my team, week in, week out, live from the Railway End Shed at Somerset Park was a step up from my usual Saturday routine. As a youngster, the highlight of my Saturdays had been my trip to the cinema in Ayr's Burns Statue Square for the weekly Odeon Club. A variety of cartoons filled the first half of the 'show' and after the interval there would be a feature length film, which invariably ended with the cavalry coming over the hill to save the day while the auditorium erupted in cheers. It couldn't compare with a full house at Somerset Park on match days but my friends and I had a great time. It may seem a little sad but I can remember every word of the Odeon Club song that we belted out during the interval every week, accompanied by the piano playing lady at the front of the picture house.

We come along on Saturday morning, greeting everybody with a smile
We come along on Saturday morning, knowing it's well worthwhile
As members of the Odeon Club we all intend to be, good citizens when we grow up and champions of the free
We come along on Saturday morning, greeting everybody with a smile, smile, smile
Greeting e-v-e-r-y-b-o-d-y with a smile.

The Old Firm fans did get one chance each season to see their team and that's when they were playing Ayr at Somerset Park. In the late sixties and early seventies Ayr United fared particularly well against Rangers but more often than not we would lose heavily to Celtic. To put things in perspective, however, Celtic won the European Cup in 1967 and Rangers lifted the European Cup Winners Cup in 1972 so we were punching well above our weight at the time. Monday morning would come around and all the arrogance and superiority that was a common trait among the armchair Celtic support would be manifested in the taunts and ridicule afforded me in the playground. In the latter years of secondary school I was subjected to ridicule on a regular basis for the crime of supporting my home town team.

Being an Ayr supporter was obviously completely different to supporting Rangers or Celtic. I doubt very much if any Old Firm fan felt such a strong affinity with their team as my fellow supporters and I experienced. A boyhood memory that has stuck with me over the years will give an insight into how intimate the relationship between players, officials and fans was at that time, although even at the smallest clubs I think things have now moved on.

The incident I speak of happened in the season Ayr won promotion back to the First Division as runners-up to Motherwell. It was in November 1968, a few weeks before my 14th birthday. It was at an Ayr United versus Forfar Athletic Second Division League match that I was right behind the goals and Forfar, shooting towards the Railway End, won a corner on the left. It was late on in the game and Ayr were coasting, 4-1 up. The crowd at the Railway End was sparse as the teams had changed ends at half-time and Ayr were shooting towards the Somerset Road end in the second half. In those days there was no segregation and the fans often swapped ends during the break. A few of us often stayed at this end so that we could have more interaction with our idols at corner kicks. The tactics employed by Ayr at defensive corners was to have the two full-backs on the posts and right-back Dick Malone, who went on to play in the Sunderland FA Cup winning team of 1973, duly took up his position inside the post as he waited for the corner kick to be taken. Dick was a big, strapping, six-foot tall defender who would go on marauding runs down the right flank with great effect. He was a fans' favourite but to be fair, at the time every player in an Ayr jersey was idolised by the supporters. These occasions gave us access to the team to an extent and we often shouted encouragement to the Ayr players. Before the ball came over I shouted to Dick Malone, 'I bet you can't score another goal before the end Dick'. To my amazement he shouted back, 'I'll bet you a penny'. The fact that one of my heroes even bothered to answer, gave me the biggest thrill. I was willing him to get a goal in the 10 minutes or so left because then I would have felt that I had played a part in the goal and the resultant 5-1 victory. I even checked my pocket to make sure I had a penny to pay my debt. Needless to say, the game ended in a 4-1 win to Ayr. At the end of the match I vaulted the perimeter wall and raced for the corner flag. There was a match day tradition at Somerset Park for youngsters to get to one of the corner flags first and if you could grab one of the flag poles before anyone else, you were allowed to carry it into the pavilion where a club official would wrest it from your grasp and chase you back out the door. On this occasion, I got a hold of the corner flagpole and hurriedly made my way into the pavilion among the players leaving the field. I spied Dick Malone entering the home dressing room and shouted after him, 'Hey Dick, you owe me a penny'. A grumpy old man grabbed the pole from me and dragged me by the collar of my jacket, to the doorway. I was about to be ejected, old Grumpy's words ringing in my ears, 'Get yersel' carted, ya cheeky wee monkey', when Dick shouted over, 'Leave the wee fella, he's right enough. Wait there till I come back out son'. The crabbit old man was not best pleased but if a player said I was to wait, he would not be overruling the decision. When the last player had gone inside the dressing room and the door closed, old Grumpy growled at me, 'Stand there and don't make a nuisance o' yersel' or you'll be oot'. The half hour wait was well worth it. Big Dick walked straight up to me, dipped his hand into his pocket and pulled out a sixpence. 'Here son, you won your bet and I'll give you 6 to 1. Is that OK?' I had no idea what he was talking about but I said 'Yes…thanks'. 'Did you enjoy the match?' said Dick. 'Brilliant,' I answered. He gave me a wink and walked away. It's difficult to tell why that meant so much to me but I was in Heaven and from that moment on, Dick Malone was my hero. I've never forgotten how kind he was to me that day and I was delighted for him when he stepped up to collect his FA Cup winners' medal at Wembley. Old Grumpy pushed me out of the front door at his first opportunity as he regained control of his prized domain but I was indifferent to his behaviour as I was floating by that time. I've been telling that story ever since. My hero. My team. If it was not already the case, I was an 'Honest Man' for life. Not only had I formed a deep affinity with my new idol, but I had also successfully embarked on my new career as a professional gambler, at the age of 13.

My Illustrious Youth Career

I may have been on cloud nine about my affinity with my hero, and my affiliation to Ayr United, but on a personal note, my opportunity to carve out a career as a player was high on my list of priorities at the time. Spring, 1969 arrived and with it the possibility of my big breakthrough.

The day had started well. I was feeling fit and although I had missed a penalty and a couple of 'sitters' the week before, my confidence was high for the Saturday morning match at Whitletts Park in Ayr against our local rivals, Decathlon Boys Club. My team, Alloway Boys Club, were sitting fifth in the under-15 league with 26 points from 18 matches and Decathlon were unbeaten, sitting proudly at the top with 32 points from the same number of games played. We were hoping to cut into their lead by ruining their record. Before the match, my coach, Alan, took me aside and told me what he expected from me. 'Gerry, I'm going to be honest with you. I'm looking for a big improvement today. Concentrate on your game because I need a special performance from you. I'll speak to you after the match.' I was not sure whether it was a compliment about my capabilities and I should feel proud or if he was giving me the proverbial 'kick up the backside' because I had not been playing well. I have to say that, whatever he meant, I felt motivated to put in a good performance and I went out onto the park with a determination to play well. The conversation that took place after our 3-0 defeat could have been directly related to the barrow-load of chances that I had missed in the match but it was more likely an indictment of my overall talent for playing football. Alan did not mince his words. 'It's simple really…' said Alan '…you're useless, by far the worst player I have ever seen. You're just not cut out for this game son. I think you should seriously consider trying something else.' There was a long pause before I realised that he was chucking me out. I was not good enough. To say that I did not get it would be an understatement of gigantic proportions. I had just been informed that I was not any good at football. 'I think you should seriously consider trying something else.' I never even enquired if it was a joke. I knew there and then that he was deadly serious. Not only was I not going to make a professional career in football but my youth club manager reckoned I was not good enough to play for the team sitting fifth in the under-15 youth league and he was advising that I should forget about playing football altogether. I had been indulging in a rather momentous case of self-delusion and I had just been brought back to earth with a thunderous crash.

Now, lesser human beings may have given up at this point but my mistake was not to wilt. Well, that is not entirely true. My determination to continue saw me enjoy playing football as a pastime in five-a-side leagues, the Ayrshire Amateur League, the West of Scotland Italian League and pub football on Sundays until I was 35 and I still look back fondly at my playing 'career' However, had I been introduced to refereeing at this point, who knows, I could have had the opportunity and honour to officiate at some of the top matches in the world, alongside some of the best teams on the planet. You will have gleaned by now that football is a passion of mine and when you are this passionate about the game, you learn to take the setbacks and make the most of it. Anyway, let us get back to the Whitletts Park prison cells, affectionately described as dressing rooms. Not for me the giddy heights of professional football. I had just been shown the door. Rejection is never a pleasant thing but I do believe that more important than the actual rejection is how you handle that rejection. I cried like a baby.

Alloway Boys Club was now behind me and I must admit, at the time

I thought my playing career was coming to a premature end. The only chance left was the school football team. Only a week after my swansong in youth club football, I was in Queen Margaret Academy's under-15 squad for a league match against Prestwick Academy…at Whitletts Park in Ayr… again. The dungeon dressing rooms were no different from the previous weekend but as I walked in I felt the disappointment, the devastation of my recent demise and I replayed the whole sorry episode in my mind. I'll be honest, I had been a substitute since the school year started and rarely did I get on the park. It was frustrating but I was able to focus more on my youth club football, so although I desperately wanted to play, I put up with being a reserve. The weather was pretty foul with the April showers deciding to come a month early. As we got changed in the dressing room, which resembled a high security prison complex, the team manager, Mr McFarlane, told me to come and see him once I was ready. This teacher was the business when it came to maths. If there was one subject I enjoyed it was maths and it was down to his teaching methods. He truly inspired me. On the football front however, his judgement was seriously flawed for the simple reason that he never picked me. That fact did not cloud my judgement of him as a teacher though. He was very, very good. So, anyway, I pulled on my light blue top with the navy collar and cuffs, the navy shorts and matching navy socks, knowing that my strips would be likely to be the only clean one left by the end of the match. Once I had laced my boots, I stepped out of the 'cell' we changed in and stepped into the next 'cell' along, which the teacher occupied on his own. He was sitting on one of the benches, hurriedly completing team lines to produce to the referee before the match started. 'Right Ferrara,' he said. For a split second I believed that Alan's words were about to be repeated to me: '…you're useless, by far the worst player I have ever seen. You're just not cut out for this game son. I think you should seriously consider trying something else'.

I could have been about to relive my weekend nightmare but my fears were unfounded. In fact, what he had to say brightened my mood considerably. 'The other boys told me you were dropped by your youth team. Today I'm giving you the whole of the second half, don't let me down.' My reply was swift, 'Thank you sir, I definitely won't let you down' and I meant it. OK, so I was substitute again but at least I was getting a game today. I felt that it was a really decent gesture of his. He did not need to give me a game, he could have left me standing at the touchline as he had done on every other occasion but this time he was coming good. The pitch was not terrific, with potholes filled with water all over the place. Having said that, the rain had eased by kick-off time and the sun had come out, it was reasonably warm. A great day for a game of football and I would be coming on for the second half.

The first half was a bit of a procession for Queen Margaret and a late goal at the end of the half made it 3-0 in our favour at the break. I was scanning the team trying to decide who would come off. I wanted to play up front but to be frank I would have taken any position. I was just desperate to get on. So, Mr McFarlane gave his half-time team talk as I waited patiently to be told who I would be replacing. His 'sermon' came and went and the players started heading back onto the pitch. Had he forgotten? He had not asked anyone to come off yet. 'Sir, where have I to play?' I asked. 'You'll need to wait a bit,' came the answer. Now, I was always respectful to this teacher, never gave him a moment's concern with my behaviour. That could have changed there and then but all I could muster was a steely stare at him. It looked like it was going to be the same old story once again but as I walked away down the touchline in a huff there was suddenly a shout. 'Oy, Ferrara, come here, quickly.' Yes! He had changed his mind, a fit of conscience no doubt. I sprinted back to the halfway line just in time to hear the referee reprimanding Mr McFarlane for his lack of efficiency in preparing his team for the second half. 'Sorry,' said the teacher to the referee. He then turned back to me and said, 'Ferrara, take your top off.' I was confused. Why would I take my strips off if I was going on? As I hesitated he shouted at me, 'Hurry up.' Whenever this teacher raised his voice to me I carried out the instructions immediately…it was a fear thing. As I was undressing I could hear from under my strips, which I was pulling over my head, that big Peter McColm was being told to take off his strips too. The teacher finally explained to me, 'He fell in that puddle and his strips is soaking, let him wear yours.' There was no protest from me, I duly handed over the strips as instructed, in exchange for a mucky strips that was saturated in dirty water. Big Peter returned to the pitch and seconds later the whistle blew for the start of the second half. I was left standing at the side of the pitch with the discarded top in my hand. My courage was developing along with my anger and probably just about matched my feeling of humiliation by this time. As Mr McFarlane turned away from me, I shouted at him, 'What am I supposed to do now?' His answer was very calm, he didn't seem annoyed that I had shouted at him, 'Just put that one on, it won't do you any harm.' I must admit that I was a trifle upset at this point and the following actions were completely out of character for me. Hard on the heels of a humiliating exit from my youth team, the ridicule I was being subjected to had been compounded by the now broken promise the teacher had given me. 'Today, I'm giving you the whole of the second half, don't let me down.' Don't let you down? Of course not! Just feel free to build up my expectations, break your promise, order me to strips in front of everyone, tell me to put on a soaking wet, filthy strips and be content to stand at the side and watch the match as I die slowly of hypothermia. While I am doing that, most importantly, I should ensure that I do not let you down. Let you down? Instead of attempting to put the strips on, I strode purposely to within a couple of yards of Mr McFarlane and initially shouted only one word. 'Sir.' He turned round to face me. I was naked from the waist up and, by the way, it was not as warm as it had been earlier. I had bundled the strips up in one hand and I could feel the water running out of it as I threw it into his face. As he reeled back he would have heard me clearly saying, 'Stick your team up your arse.' I then marched to the pavilion where the jail warden, the building caretaker, had been watching events unfold. He silently unlocked the door and let me in to change my clothes. On the way out I thanked him and slung my bag over my shoulder. Without the slightest glance in the direction of the teacher, I stomped off to start the half-mile walk home, feeling sorry for myself. Two careers down inside a week and you could be forgiven for thinking I would crumble. Well, after thinking about it rationally...I cried like a baby.

A four-year period away from organised football followed my two big disappointments. Alan's opinion had been corroborated by Mr McFarlane's assessment of my ability. I was useless. Strangely enough, I was not worried about facing the music when I went back into school. I had been wronged and I would be standing up to him. Although I had a feeling I would be getting into trouble that day, I need not have worried. Mr McFarlane acted as if nothing had happened. I had assaulted a teacher and he decided to take no action. Looking back, I am in no doubt that it was his conscience that guided him in his lack of action. It is quite peculiar how some adults think it is alright to abuse children. As long as the adult gets things the way he or she wants, how the child feels is apparently unimportant. It is psychological abuse and it's not nice.

So, my youth team had discarded me and having resigned from the school team in a huff, I was at a loose end. Salvation however, was just around the corner and something positive was about to happen. With nothing remotely interesting in my life, other than a kick about in the small grassed area at the bottom of Dunlop Terrace, I decided to join the school youth club. I had only been going for a couple of weeks when Mr McFarlane, yes the same one, was pinning up a list of four people who were in the Youth Club team that would be competing in the Ayr Table Tennis Singles Championship the following weekend. I had been playing table tennis at school all year, thanks to a lunchtime arrangement me and a few friends had with Mr McPate, the PE teacher. He allowed us to play at lunchtimes in the dressing room area beside the boys' gym and we never gave him any problems. There were usually four of us and I played a lot of table tennis, developing a bit of an aptitude for the game over that period. I had an attacking style that worked well for me alongside some nice spin I could put on the ball. I surveyed the sheet on the notice board and reckoned I could beat all of the players on the list. Bobby McGaffney was the only player at the school who was exceptional, much better than me. He was not in our team because he never attended our youth club. Not that it made any difference. I would not be playing in the competition so it was all irrelevant. It was fair enough. I had not been at the club for very long and it would have been wrong to replace someone who had merited their place on the team. Mr McFarlane saw me eyeing up the details and he said that although I was not in the team I could come along as a reserve and play if someone could not make it. Déjà vu, you might think. Do not even consider it you may advise. I never needed to be asked twice, 'Yes sir, I'll come.' The competition was being held in a place called the Phoenix Halls in Russell Street if I remember correctly. I was told to be there for 9.30am on the following Saturday and I arrived 20 minutes early. As the competitors filtered in I watched for any sign of my youth club colleagues. Two arrived together followed by another five minutes later. By the 10 o'clock start time number four had not arrived. Mr McFarlane broke the good news that I was in the team. I had my own table tennis bat with me, a cherished Christmas present. It was a slightly padded bat covered with a soft rubber outer layer. It had no dimples on the surface and it looked impressive with its oak coloured handle. I was raring to go. The draw was announced and the format for the competition was knockout, best of three games to 21 points. We got together as a team before the start and Mr McFarlane gave us a pep talk before we went to our allocated tables to start. I actually sat out the first group of matches as there were not enough tables to play all the first round matches. I was walking around the hall eyeing up the opposition playing on the eight tables when I spied Bobby McGaffney. He was there to represent Mossblown Youth Club and he had started his first round match. I stayed around to watch him trounce his opponent, who barely won a point and lost the first two games in double-quick time. The poor boy would be going home sooner than he would have wanted. Then it was my turn. Nerves took over and I struggled in my first game, losing 21-15. I calmed down after that and won the next two games comfortably. My opponent was really graceful in defeat and his parting shot was, 'I hope you win the competition. Then I can say that I lost to the winner'.

It was going to be a good day now. Even if I had lost in the next round I would have gone home happy. I had competed and I had won. As the tournament progressed I grew in confidence and by three o'clock in the afternoon I found myself lining up against Bobby McGaffney in the final. He was much too good for me in the first game and he won 21-9. The second game of the best of three final went my way, 21-16, and the reason for that was Bobby's arrogance and complacency. The deciding game was going as planned for McGaffney until I happened on a defensive strategy that paid dividends. My opponent smashed a drive down the middle of the table and instead of trying to smash the ball back I just put forward a straight bat to defend it. To my surprise the ball flew to the back of the table and beat him all ends up. The next point saw another big smash flying towards me. My straight bat sent the ball careering back over the net and past his forehand to win me another point. His frustration turned to anger and he started flailing at the ball and missing his shots. We arrived at 19-19 and now I had a genuine chance of winning. I blocked his next shot and the ball skidded on his side of the table and past his bat. With the pressure of facing a match point, Bobby served into the net and, unbelievably, I had won the tournament. I admit here and now, he was a much, much better player than me but my defensive tactics had worked and somehow I was the 1970 Ayr and District Table Tennis Champion. 'I told you anything was possible,' said my mentor, who had apparently forgiven me for the face-full of filthy, wet football strips that I had given him to signal the end of my school football career. 'I told you anything was possible,' he repeated.

Nah, you never did anything of the kind sir. Not that I would ever have the courage to say such a thing. He never rated me as a footballer or a table tennis player. The fact is that he abused his power and exploited my weakness on the side of the football pitch that day. It was a nasty thing to do. He was gracious enough to let me come to the table tennis tournament though. That was a really nice gesture. The thing that tips the balance in Mr McFarlane's favour was that he was a brilliant teacher, so I do not want to be too critical of him.

My glorious win meant that I was appointed Captain of the Ayr and District team that was to compete in the up and coming Ayrshire Finals to be held at Mainholm Academy the following month. Football? Who needs it? Table tennis is the future. Well, that was until the Ayrshire finals in May. Each of our team, the four semi-finalists from the Ayr and District Championships, played two matches at the county finals and we never won a game. In the best of three matches, I lost convincingly to a boy from Saltcoats before being hammered by a Dalmellington player. Table tennis? It's a stupid, stupid game. My ping-pong career was short and glorious to an extent. It did not take me long though to discover that I was not very good at it. I was useless at football and pitiful at table tennis. Oh for some saving grace, something to raise me from my pathetic life of boredom and underachievement.

The summer of '69 did offer some excitement and a world event that captured my imagination was the American moon landing in July. At 3 o'clock on the morning of 21 July, my father let me down badly. The evening before, he had agreed that if I went to my bed early he would come upstairs and get me out of bed to watch the first astronaut walking on the moon's surface when the time came. I woke up the next morning to find that Neil Armstrong had made history while I was sleeping. My dad always swore that he tried to get me up but that I had turned over and gone back to sleep. I never did believe him.

Touching Glory

The 1969-70 football season is one that made an indelible mark on my mind. If I could present a gift to a younger generation of Ayr United supporters, it would be time travel back to that period to experience that wonderful, wonderful season. Although we at Ayr United have never experienced glory in its truest recognised form of cups and medals, we have had our moments and I was there to see some of the best.

On the morning of the 8 October 1969 a momentous occasion was upon us. As a 14-year-old, nothing in the world was more important than this. Ayr United were within touching distance of our very first national Cup Final. All that stood in our way was a Celtic side that had triumphed over Inter Milan in Lisbon 17 months previously, to assume the title of European Champions. Not only that, but this was a Celtic team that would go on, seven months later, to contest yet another European Cup Final against Feyenoord of Holland. The supporters of any provincial club would be justified in fearing the worst on a morning like this but we were not your run of the mill football supporters. What separated our club from other small teams was our inspirational leader. If Ally MacLeod said we were good enough, well that was also good enough for every Ayr supporter, me included. The most charismatic figure in Ayr United's history had been 'banging the drum' for his team well in advance of the tie and declaring to anyone who would listen that our wee club was afraid of no team. The height of my optimism that morning was directly related to Ally's arrogance and self-assurance. He instilled in our players a self-belief that no other manager could have articulated with so much effect. I hung on his every word and I thirsted for any scrap of a statement from our Messiah. His confidence shone through his team. It showed in the way Ayr United played. In the late sixties and in the seventies, Somerset Park was a ground that no team wanted to come to. The stultifying, boring tactics associated with teams playing against either of the Old Firm at that time or to this day is not a label that could be hung on Ayr United. MacLeod set out his teams to win. He would attack from the start and against Rangers or Celtic it made for fast, attractive, open football that is now a rarity in the Scottish game. My team did more than their share to ensure top class entertainment and we, the Ayr supporters, were the main beneficiaries.

I could not think straight. The very idea of going head to head with the Scottish League Champions with the possibility of my team making history by appearing in the League Cup Final filled me with an equal measure of exhilaration and anticipation. On the day of the match I was up early and went downstairs, stopped at the bottom stair and sat there staring at the letter box, patiently waiting for the *Daily Record* to pop through and land on the carpet. As soon as it hit the floor, I grabbed it and ran quickly through to the living room, laying the paper face down on the coffee table. After scanning the back page for any mention of the game, I turned it over to reveal the inside pages and I sat forward on the couch, leaning over the headlines and taking in every bit of information the words could provide me with. The bold capitals of the headline relating to the match read;

'AYR PROMISE A HAMPDEN CLASSIC'

The article was exactly what I needed, as the confidence exuded by Ally MacLeod reinforced what I knew already. We were on the brink of making club history. 'I know my boys and I know if they play to top form they can beat Celtic,' said Ally. The thing is, MacLeod may have been perceived as boastful and arrogant to some and eccentric and laughable to others but his assertions were not mere bluster. The results achieved by our small provincial club backed up his rhetoric. He was charismatic and was able to motivate not only the players but the fans too. I never believed that we would lose the match. I was sure that victory was ours for the taking, despite the fact that wee Ayr United were facing the might of Europe. Delusional? Not me.

By the time I arrived at Ayr train station, I was beside myself with excitement. It was 5 o'clock and the 'football special' would be leaving at half past five. There was a fair crowd of people already mingling on the platform, most bedecked in their black and white scarves but a few green and white clad supporters joined the waiting throng to take advantage of the cheap train journey to King's Park. One hour after the train departed, followed by a 15-minute walk to the national stadium and we were paying our 2s 6d to take our place at the 'Rangers End' of the ground. We were in among a crowd of about 1,000 Ayr supporters on the terrace, under the covered enclosure. As the 35,000 paying customers filed into the stadium, we were eventually surrounded by Celtic supporters but in much the same way as our home match against Rangers a month earlier, there was no trouble. Looking around the stadium, there were pockets of Ayr United supporters in every part of the ground belting out our repertoire of songs. We had, '*Viva Bobby Rough*', sung in honour of our left-winger to the tune of the Equals' *Viva Bobby Joe* It was a number six hit in the 1969 charts at the end of August and it was quickly adapted for our purposes.

> '*Bobby Rough...Viva Bobby Rough*
> *Bobby Rough...Viva Bobby Rough*
> *Viva...Viva*
> *Viva Bobby Rough...VIVA*
> *Bobby Rough and his goal machine...*' etc.

It was simple but effective. Another big hit of the sixties came in handy to show our admiration for our hard man at centre-half, Stan Quinn. Although Manfred Mann had topped the charts with the song in 1968, the Ayr supporters adopted it and kept it going throughout Stan Quinn's time at the club.

'Come on without…Come on within
You'll not see nothin' like the Mighty Quinn
Come on without…Come on within
You'll not see nothin' like the Stanley Quinn.'

Then there was the long-winded *We've Got The Best Team In The Land*, which involved singing a verse for every player in the team. When Obie Phillis wrote, *He's got the Whole World in His Hands,* during World War Two he would not have had an inkling that it would be sung from the terraces at Somerset Park and beyond. The thing is, it was a gospel song and we were spreading the word of our heroes wherever we went. I'm sure he would have approved. I must admit to the fact that by the time we had reached Dougie Mitchell at number six, it did start to get a bit monotonous.

'We've got Davie Stewart, number 1 (3 times)
We've got the best team in the land
We've got Dick Malone, number 2 (3 times)
We've got the best team in the land, etc, etc'

The Ayr 'choir' was in excellent form. It was a cold night and as the teams ran out the floodlights highlighted the thick fog that hung over the stadium. Fortunately, the fog never interrupted the match and by the time the game kicked off it had cleared just as if the curtain was coming up on the drama that was to follow. In terms of excitement, pleasure, drama, exhilaration, fear and despair, it was all there on the evening of Wednesday 8 October and it exceeded all my expectations. Quite simply, it was the greatest night ever to be an Ayr United supporter.

Ally MacLeod stuck to his guns with an all-out attacking strategy. The expectation was that Celtic would do their own share of attacking but the hard working Ayr forwards would be tutored well in adapting to defensive roles when required. I have never witnessed time pass as quickly as I did that night. The first half was over in a flash and it had gone well for Ayr.

I can recall vividly the 32nd minute of the match when Ayr went ahead. It was 'Cutty' Young who whipped the ball into the box and when Bobby Rough planted his header in the back of the net, my head felt like it would explode at any second. The Celtic supporters in the 33,110 crowd fell silent as groups of Ayr fans, spattered around the ground, celebrated wildly. My stomach was churning, I was delirious with joy and there and then I was certain that we would go on and win the match.

'It had been previewed as an execution, a goals jamboree, and a walkover, but the spectators were quickly to change their minds,' said the match report in the *Glasgow Herald* on 9 October.

This was a talented Celtic side however and when 'Yogi' Hughes equalised for Celtic just before half-time, my stomach was churning for a completely different reason. I could not contemplate Ayr losing and the very idea that Celtic would score again made me feel nauseous. It had been end-to-end football for 45 minutes and if anything, Ayr had the better of the play. Nothing to fear, Ally MacLeod would have the team pumped up for the second half. They were indeed and the team continued to make good openings. The Ayr wingers were running their opponents ragged and Alex 'Dixie' Ingram was giving Billy McNeil a torrid time with his physical play. When Celtic took the lead I started having doubts, particularly as the goal should never have been. John 'Spud' Murphy tackled Willie Wallace inside the Ayr penalty area and Wallace went down like a Saturday pools coupon and the referee was conned. He gave a penalty and in the 50th minute Tommy Gemmell put Celtic ahead from the spot. I was angry at the injustice but I can honestly say that I never lost heart. Ayr were still pushing forward and justice was done 10 minutes later when 'Dixie' Ingram pulled Billy McNeil to the ground with him as wee Davy McCulloch ran clear to drill the ball home for the equaliser; extra-time it was. Ayr United had held the League champions over 90 minutes and they intended to finish the job in the 30 minutes to follow. Bobby Rough popped up again, five minutes into extra-time, and we were 3-2 up. Our crowd were delirious. We were convinced that we were going through. Nobody could take this away from us now. Unfortunately, three minutes later, and despite the magnificent Davie Stewart in goal, Bertie Auld managed to squeeze a shot just inside the post to beat the big 'keeper. Celtic had pulled the game out of the fire to earn a replay.

A 3-3 draw against Celtic in the semi-final of the 1969 League Cup. Victory had been within our grasp and although we had watched in agony as our lead slipped away at the death, I was mightily proud of my team's display. Do not be kidded, this was not a hanging on, scraped draw against the giants of Europe. No, we had taken the game to Celtic at every opportunity, we had hurt them and if not for that Bertie Auld strike, we would have beaten them…deservedly. It had been such an energy sapping experience on the Wednesday and three days later there was still a small matter of travelling to Tannadice Park in Dundee for a First Division match against Dundee United on the Saturday. As if that was not difficult enough, Ayr would then need to return to Glasgow two days later to do battle once more with Celtic in the replay to finally get what we deserved…our place in the Final of the League Cup against St Johnstone. Wednesday, Saturday, Monday. With a 12-man squad (only one substitute in those days) of part-time players, I think it is fair to say that Ayr United were punching above their weight. Nevertheless, there were no complaints emanating from Somerset Park about having to play three games in six days. The management, the players and the supporters were totally focused on the job in hand and everyone played their part. Saturday arrived and understandably Ayr struggled against Dundee United, finally going down 3-1. Were the team tired? Well, I was not at Dundee because of a financial problem. My mother had explained, 'Money doesn't grow on trees. If you're going back to Glasgow on Monday you can forget about Dundee'. On the morning of that match with Dundee United, Ally MacLeod was at it again. He announced his 'Lucky Thirteen' hypothesis and the *Daily Record's* back page carried the headline 'IT'S LUCKY THIRTEEN FOR MACLEOD'S MEN'. The Alex Cameron article was based on three very tenuous links that suggested an omen for the outcome of the second match with Celtic. 'We will replay Celtic on Monday the THIRTEENTH which is great for us,' said Ally, 'It was September the THIRTEENTH that we beat Rangers at Somerset and Wednesday was my THIRTEENTH wedding anniversary.' I fully concurred with Ally Macleod but it wasn't just because of the omen. Based on the performance in the first game and the display delivered one month earlier, in a League match against the mighty Rangers at Somerset Park, I had every reason to believe that we could go to Hampden and turn over Celtic at the second time of asking.

The date 13 September 1969 will live forever in my memory as another of those great Ayr United performances. I respect the fact that some people older than me will have memories that pre-date my time supporting the team but if they witnessed a better display from our team, than I did on that particular Saturday, they are lucky, lucky people. Whenever I recall the events of that day, the hairs on the back of my neck stand to attention, I get a lump in my throat and tears of joy are never far away. I would have been happy to describe this experience as my greatest ever Ayr United experience if it was not for the League Cup semi-final that followed only a month later but nevertheless the Rangers match is right up there, as far as memorable matches go. I was in Tryfield Place by 1pm that day and I was not alone. The turnstiles would not be opening till half past one but I stood patiently in the long queue, with four of my friends, waiting for admittance into the Railway End of the ground. When the doors to the turnstiles finally opened, a big roar went up from the two hundred or so who had gathered impatiently at the far end of Tryfield Place. The street in those days was quite different from today. Opposite the main entrance for players and officials was an old terrace of flatted properties and the view the occupiers got from their front windows was the back of a big, ugly football stand. I always felt a real atmosphere in the narrow street, especially when there was a throng of excited supporters ahead of a big match. There was no such thing as segregation and supporters of both teams mingled together both outside and inside the ground. After negotiating my entry onto the terrace, I was able to choose my spot. Our group of friends made for a favoured spot directly behind the goals and right at the front, against the perimeter wall. It meant that nothing or nobody blocked our view and we were as close to the pitch as anyone could get. At least, that is what I thought. As it happened, I was going to be a whole lot nearer to the action than I had anticipated. The closer we got to the 3 o'clock kick-off time, the more the pressure grew behind us. The number of people in Somerset Park was incredible, far and away the biggest crowd I had ever been part of. Quarter to three and I could not see a space in the entire ground. The fans who made up the Ayr 'choir' were working their way through their repertoire of songs and chants but the Rangers support was growing in numbers behind them, higher up the terracing. Slowly but surely the crowd was being forced ever further towards the front. It was becoming really uncomfortable for me, pressed hard against the wall at the front. My face was getting redder and redder. The combination of the warm September sunshine and the congestion in the 'shed' was making life very difficult for those of us at the front. The next thing I knew, people were climbing over the four-foot wall at the front of the crowd and they were spilling onto the blaise track that ran around the side of the pitch. I decided to do the same and a policeman actually helped me to get over. To be fair to the police, they had realised that there were too many fans in the ground and they relieved the congestion by sensibly managing a mini pitch invasion. Under the supervision of the officers, the predominantly young supporters who had vaulted the wall were instructed to sit on the grass behind the goal line. The same was happening all around the pitch and it was right up my street. My prime position was on the junction of the six-yard box with the goal line. I had an unobstructed view of the playing area for the biggest match of my life. It does not get any better than this. Only when the crowd was settled in their positions, did the teams appear. The roar that greeted them was louder than anything I had heard before. As the teams lined up, ready to start, the noise built into a crescendo. I could hardly hear myself think. The crowd record for Somerset Park was broken that day. 25,225 people squeezed into the stadium and the terracing could not cope. With the benefit of hindsight, it was folly to allow that many people to enter the ground. When one thinks of disasters that were to follow in subsequent years at Ibrox, Valley Parade, Heysel and Hillsborough, this day that I still remember fondly could have been catastrophic. Not that I was aware of it, I was having the time of my life. We did not have high wire fences, there was no particular animosity from supporters towards one another and the police used common sense to control a generally good-natured crowd. The disasters I alluded to could not be described in the same way and in this respect, I suppose we were all very lucky that day, but in more ways than one. We were treated to a feast of attacking football that is sadly missing from Scottish football nowadays.

The good news was that Ayr were able to field their strongest 11;

Stewart, Malone, Murphy, Fleming, Quinn, Mitchell, Young, Ferguson, Ingram, McCulloch, Rough.

It was not just the strongest 11 of that season. In my opinion, it was Ayr United's greatest ever team, certainly in my 45 years of supporting the team. Every one of them contributed significantly, every one of them capable of something special. More importantly, they were a wonderful team that complemented one another so well. It would have been understandable if, on the day, the occasion had got to Ayr's part-timers. After all, they were facing players with big reputations. The names, Greig, Jardine, Baxter, Johnston and Stein trip off the tongue easily and will still be instantly recognisable to most fans even 40 years on from that special match.

However, as I mentioned, this was Ayr United's greatest ever team. They were nerveless.

Ayr United would be defending the Railway End goal in the first half and as soon as the game started, they took the game to Rangers. The Glasgow giants were tentative in their approach and Ayr United players were snapping into their tackles. If the Ibrox club had any notion that our wee team would roll over, they would already have had an unpleasant surprise. MacLeod's strategy was clear. Do not give them any time on the ball, close them down early and when we get the ball, go for the jugular. Ayr enjoyed a lion's share of the possession in the early stages and Gerry Neef, Rangers' German goalkeeper, had a busy opening spell. Quintin 'Cutty' Young, a very gifted player with a magical left foot, took up his position on the right wing and panic broke out in the Rangers defence every time he took possession of the ball. It may seem strange that he was Ayr's outside-right but Ayr had another terrific winger on the left flank. Bobby Rough was a player with great ball control and a devastating turn of foot.

He was also a prolific goalscorer. Ally MacLeod had made room for both in his team by switching Young to the right, where he was probably a bigger threat. His speciality was taking the ball on the touchline and running straight at the full-back. He would twist and turn before cutting inside and shooting with his lethal left foot. That is exactly what he did that day. After 23 minutes he took on the left-back, dropped his shoulder and cut inside his opponent. Before the Rangers defender had time to recover, Young unleashed a thunderbolt left foot drive and the ball flew high into the net as Neef tried in vain to get across his goal to block the shot. It felt like an electric shock was running through my body. I was up on my feet celebrating on the pitch. It was only when a policeman started ushering me and another 50 youngsters back to our places on the goal line that I realised that I had been celebrating on the pitch. Before the drama of the opening goal, the Somerset Road End of the ground had been a virtual sea of blue, red and white, packed full of Rangers fans singing, chanting and roaring their team on. The hammer blow of going a goal behind changed that picture completely. The spectators on the open terracing behind the Rangers goal stood in stunned silence, like cardboard cut-outs, as the Ayr players mobbed the scorer, the hero of the moment. Take a bow 'Cutty' Young, you are indeed a genius. The Ayr supporters behind me in the Railway End were hysterical and there were pockets of 'Honest Men' all around the ground jumping up and down as the Rangers supporters beside them stood motionless, shocked and bewildered.

It would be foolish to believe that Rangers would not come back strongly but the fact was that we were in the driving seat and at no time during this match did my team look as if they would relinquish their lead. A deserved second goal arrived after 38 minutes when Jackie Ferguson, Ayr's inside-right, finished off a great move by stabbing the ball home. Cue more hysteria. In all my 14 years I had never experienced anything like this. The atmosphere in the ground was euphoric, the excitement had reached fever pitch. The quality of football on display was first class. Ayr's fast moving, passing game was a joy to watch. The entire first half seemed to be about Ayr United pressing forward, looking for goals. Or maybe that is just the skewed perception of a sycophantic black and white army recruit from the victorious Somerset squadron. Facts are facts however. Ayr were two goals up at half-time and Rangers would have their work cut out trying to claw their way back into the match.

The second half saw no quarter given and both teams did their utmost to attack at every opportunity. Towards the end of the match Ayr did begin to tire and to be fair to Rangers they piled on the pressure. Ayr's defence however was more than capable of coping with everything Rangers could throw at them. The pleasure derived by every Ayr supporter in the ground, in relation to the scoreline, was to be enhanced even further when the Ayr players began showboating and teasing their opponents. With the clock running down, Davie Stewart, the Ayr goalkeeper, rolled the ball out to Dick Malone at right-back. The defender played the ball from foot to foot before returning it to his 'keeper. Stewart picked the ball up and rolled it out to left-back John Murphy who repeated Malone's antics and when Stewart collected it for the second time he simply turned towards Malone and started the whole process over again. The Rangers players stood back for an inordinate amount of time as if they were unsure what to do. We were lapping it up. Here we were, taking the Mickey out of the mighty Glasgow Rangers. This was fun. I believe that Rangers pulling a goal back in the last minute of the match was due more to the arrogance being displayed by the Ayr players than any great play by the away team. Nevertheless, having made the score 2-1, Colin Stein was quick to collect the ball from the back of the net before sprinting back to the centre circle for the game to be restarted. He clearly believed that his team could still salvage a point. He was wrong. The final whistle sounded and the home supporters continued with the singing and dancing that would last long into the night. Both points went to Ayr United and they were richly deserved.

As I left the ground, quite a scary experience in the crush going back down Tryfield Place, I was in a daze. Ally MacLeod had masterminded a great victory against the elite of the Scottish First Division. I was bursting with pride thanks to the performance of every Ayr United player who took part in that great victory. The result of that match, coupled with the experience I had lived through on the day, sustained my dream-like state for weeks after and although the high standards of 13 September were not maintained in our subsequent League matches, the team still managed to finish 14th in the League that season. It had been a success. We were newly promoted and held our place in the top division comfortably.

Of course, the 1969-70 season never started on 13 September. The excitement of promotion from the Second Division the previous season brought with it the anticipation of top-level football against top-level opposition. I would say that although I was a willing conscript to the MacLeod doctrine, it was not entirely blind faith. Our leader, and his players, had produced hard evidence that we were capable of beating any team at Fortress Somerset. The first League match of that season took place on Saturday 30 August and it was a mouth-watering introduction to the top division with a home match against Hibernian. On this occasion, I stood right in the middle of the terrace, directly behind the goals at the Railway End. The terracing steps had not been concreted over at that stage and a feature of the goal celebrations in that part of the ground was the cloud of dust that rose from between the railway sleepers, laid side by side and used as terracing steps, as the Ayr support jumped up and down after each of the goals. By the end of the game my clothes were filthy and my face was more akin to an emerging miner from a pit. Ayr blew away the opposition with a 3-0 victory and Scottish football sat up and took notice. Four days later, the team travelled through to Dunfermline and earned another point with a commendable 0-0 draw. I will concede that the Rangers match was an altogether bigger challenge but the foundations had been laid for the triumph to follow with the solid start to the League campaign. The 2-1 humbling of Rangers was in no way a flash in the pan. We were a match for any of the 'big boys' but despite all the early season success the team had achieved, it was probably too big a task for them to pull off a replay victory against Celtic at Hampden Park on the Monday night.

On the morning of the replay with Celtic I was still full of the euphoria developed from the first match. The way I looked at it, any lingering doubts about our team's capability to beat Celtic had dissipated. We had taken them to the brink and they had stolen a draw. All we had to do was finish the job. The train journey up to Glasgow was loud and there was an air of positivity and even celebration among the Ayr fans. News of an injury to Bobby Rough had filtered through to the supporters and if he had been ruled out it would have been a big blow to the team. However, the team entered the arena and Bobby Rough took his usual place in the line up. Despite the fact that the team had endured a really hectic schedule of matches, MacLeod named an unchanged line up for the match. We never had the strength in depth that the Old Firm had but hopefully our players would manage one more big effort to take us into the League Cup Final.

The replay was perhaps not as exciting as the first match but Ayr once again gave a good account of themselves. Our team's positive start to the match paid a dividend when Alex Ingram rattled in a goal after 14 minutes and we had another couple of chances before Harry Hood equalised eight minutes later. Our League Cup campaign hinged on two incidents in this match that illustrate perfectly, the fine line between success and failure. Early in the second half, Stan Quinn, a most dependable defender, made the most horrendous blunder right in front of his own goal. When the ball dropped at his feet, instead of clearing his lines he appeared to be caught in two minds and he played the ball into the path of Stevie Chalmers, who duly slipped the ball into the net for what turned out to be the winner. As was always the case with this Ayr team, they battled back and when Alex Ingram directed his header towards goal, I raised my arms to greet the goal but somehow Ronnie Simpson managed to dive full length to block the ball down at his post. The reward for his heroics was a dislocated shoulder but a place for his team in the League Cup Final later that month. Tommy Gemmell replaced him in goal and Ally MacLeod could be seen on the touchline, waving his team forward and urging them to force a way past the big defender. Ayr could not find a way through. It was all over. Glorious defeat was the result but there was no way my love for the game and for my team would diminish. I was an 'Honest Man' for life.

The train was eerily quiet on the way back home. There would have been no sound at all but for half a dozen of us crying into our scarves as we made our way back home, dejected. An old man sitting across the carriage tried to console us, 'Never mind boys, it's only a game of football'. A young guy, maybe about a couple of years older than me, sitting directly opposite my seat, looked up. His eyes were red and filled with tears. All he could muster up as a reply was, 'Oh mister...' as he put his head in his hands and continued weeping inconsolably.

We would have murdered St Johnstone in the Final.

Life, Death and Scumbags

On 14 October 1969 I came back down to earth with a bump. I was back at school on that Tuesday morning to face all the taunts from those marvellous Celtic supporters who revelled in my misery. There was an altogether more worrying situation I would need to deal with in the months ahead however. My birthday was fast approaching, I would be 15 on 8 December and I had major decisions to make. Stay on at school? Leave and find a job? Go to college? I was about to grow up fast, whether I liked it or not. The only interest I had in life was football and I was hardly going to make a living as a football fan. My mum insisted that I stay on at school. I insisted that I would be leaving. I hated secondary school and could not wait for the Christmas holidays. That would be my first chance to get out of there for good and I intended to grasp the opportunity with both hands.

The school leaving age was raised to 16 in 1972 so I made it with a bit to spare. If I'm honest, although I did not want to remain at school, I was very apprehensive about adult life and having to work for a living and I certainly did not want to go to college. College it was then. My mum took my immaturity into account and made up my mind for me. I was enrolled on a Pre-Apprenticeship course at Ayr Technical College. The one-year course was designed to give school leavers an opportunity to sample construction trades and develop skills to enhance employment opportunities as Apprentice Joiners, Bricklayers, Plumbers, Slaters and Painters and Decorators. I was not enthusiastic but anything would be better than staying at Queen Margaret Academy. After enjoying the Christmas holidays, I started on my college course in January and soon discovered that I was not the type to get my hands dirty. So straight away that ruled out, well, just about everything. Painting and decorating was almost tolerable and I managed to do enough in the other subjects to achieve my course certificate. During my time at college, more importantly, Ayr United consolidated their place in the First Division, finishing 14th and there was a bonus in the shape of beating Killie twice. A 3-2 League win at Somerset in January was followed in April by a 2-0 win in the Ayrshire Cup Final. All things considered, it had been a good season.

By Christmas 1970, Somerset Park had already taken delivery of some new furniture. We were looking very professional with our newly installed floodlights perched on four massive pylons, one in each corner of the ground. The lights seemed to breathe new life into the club. A challenge match took place in November to celebrate the inauguration of the new floodlights and Ayr recorded a 2-0 win over Newcastle United. The floodlights confirmed our status as a team on the up. We were one of the big boys now, competing in the First Division and able to beat anyone, day or night.

Fast-forward to 31 May 2011 and the same floodlights disappeared from the local landscape. A mixture of neglect and rust had taken its toll and the giants were felled within a few days. It was the end of an era and I can admit to having a lump in my throat when I saw some of the pictures a fellow 'mourner' had posted on the fans forum section of the 'Honest Page', Ayr United fans' unofficial Internet site. As United supporters back in the day, we had all contributed small amounts of money towards the cost of those floodlights and there was a certain feeling of pride in that 'achievement'. Some marvellous nights were enjoyed under the light provided by those four giants and after 41 years they did not owe us a penny.

Floodlight inauguration aside, it was not exactly Ayr's most auspicious period in their history and when compared to the trials and tribulations of the 1969-70 season's successful joust with Rangers and glorious failure against

Celtic, it was not the most riveting time to be an Ayr fan. Nevertheless, Ayr United had consolidated their position in the top division with 14th place for a second season. If only we could replicate the standards of the early seventies today, in terms of quality players and entertainment levels, we would be in a very good place indeed. In the words of a 1970 song by Joni Mitchell '*You don't know what you've got till it's gone*'.

Christmas 1970 was also an important time for me on a personal basis. My college course was almost complete and I found myself applying to local businesses for an apprenticeship. Hugh Law of John Law & Sons, a Prestwick company, gave me my big chance. I was not particularly enthusiastic about my appointment but on Wednesday 6 January 1971, I embarked on my long and illustrious career as a painter and decorator. On the Friday before I started with John Law & Sons, it was New Year's Day. Ayr were at home and a 2-1 win against Morton set us up nicely for the away trip to Kilmarnock the following day but I was not going to be there. I had no money and my dad reckoned a wee rest from the football would do me good. My protest that a derby match could not be missed fell on deaf ears. Apparently, I needed a rest before embarking on my lifelong career path in the decorating industry.

So, there I was, stuck at home with the only consolation being the Grandstand Teleprinter on the BBC typing away furiously providing the full-time results as they came into the studio. It was a nervy experience, watching every letter or digit appearing on the screen individually. Do not ask me where everyone was that afternoon but I remember clearly that I was home alone. While Ayr were earning a 1-1 draw against Kilmarnock at Rugby Park, Rangers and Celtic were at Ibrox for the Old Firm derby. It was a Saturday like no other. I never heard how Ayr fared until much later in the evening and that was because of events unfolding in Glasgow. As I anxiously waited for my team's result there was an interruption to the programme. An announcement was made by the presenter that there had been an 'incident' at Ibrox Park in Glasgow. After a couple of minutes, the announcer came back on to say that it was a serious incident and some people had been hurt. Eventually the programme switched to pictures at the stadium and I watched in disbelief as police, supporters and club officials used makeshift stretchers to carry the injured, dying and dead onto the pitch. The horror associated with that afternoon will always be etched on my mind. I watched the disastrous outcome as dead bodies were laid side by side along one of the goal lines. I had nobody sitting with me, nobody to talk to, to share the gut-wrenching sight of people dying for a stupid football match. I was completely overwhelmed by the pictures and the commentator's dour, monotone voice betraying a sense of hopelessness. The tears were rolling down my cheeks and I was in a state of shock at the events. I did not really care at the time whether Ayr had won or not. That night, I did not really care about football at all. It goes without saying that the game I love is not worth one person's life, never mind that of 66 people. For every one of them there was a family who would be bereaved, who would be devastated. People do not die at football matches but they did that day. It is only now that I can relate the appalling loss of life to my own experiences on the terracing. I can look back fondly to Ayr United's 2-1 victory against Rangers in 1969 but things could have gone terribly wrong that day. The official crowd statistic from that match was 25,225 but some would argue there were many more than that inside Somerset Park. Was it safe? Well, the fact that a large number of youngsters were forced to clamber over the perimeter wall and sit at the side of the pitch would suggest that the safety of the spectators was compromised to accommodate a crowd that exceeded the capacity of the ground. The circumstances of the Ibrox disaster cannot be compared with those at the 1969 Ayr United versus Rangers match. There were 100,000 plus at the Rangers versus Celtic match, so the scale is different but it is true to say that there were many matches before 1971 that could have ended in catastrophe and the misfortune of Glasgow Rangers and everyone connected with the club could have been visited upon any club at the time. To use a well-worn cliché of footballers, 'at the end of the day'…we are all football fans, we are all the same. Or are we?

In a civilised society, one would think that we would all show some compassion for others in their time of grief but we perhaps do not live in a fully civilised society. The grief associated with the Ibrox disaster is not shared by some people and although they may be in a small minority, the moronic antics of some imbeciles in our country in the present day, shames all football supporters. As I carried out some research for this book, I came across a video recording posted on 'YouTube' I had been looking at tributes to Ibrox disaster victims and a video entitled, 'Celtic Fans Mocking the Ibrox Disaster' caught my eye. The participants in the singsong on a supporter's bus engaged in mocking the dead of 1971 before moving on to express their glee about the untimely death of Davie Cooper, the former Rangers winger. In truth, they are not Celtic supporters. They are merely morons who have attached themselves to the club. I am in no doubt that Celtic would do anything they could to disassociate themselves with these low-lifes. All clubs have an undesirable element but it would be wonderful if we could eradicate this scum from our national game. The reasoning behind allowing vile content like this on the 'YouTube' site is lost on me.

My weekend passed, an away point for Ayr was my prize and the price was 66 fellow football fans. I could say that it was a weekend to forget but I would rather put it like this. It was a weekend to remember. I do not want to forget about the victims of the Ibrox disaster or any of the other catastrophes that were to follow in subsequent years. Valley Parade, Heysel, Hillsborough. Is our obsession with football worth the losses suffered in Glasgow, Bradford, Brussels and Sheffield? It sickens me to think that people can find humour in these disasters. There is always someone who takes great delight in telling jokes at the expense of people who have either lost their lives or who live their lives in despair at the loss of a loved one. When I think about the rivalry that exists between the fans of opposing clubs, I wonder if it is too much to ask for a bit of perspective. I have always been very passionate about my team but my experience has taught me that there are more important things in life than football. I want Ayr United to win every game and while I am very disappointed when they lose, it is not more important than life or death. It may have been a tongue in cheek comment, but if Bill Shankly had lived to witness the Hillsborough tragedy, he would surely have retracted that famous statement: 'Football's not a matter of life and death…it's more important than that.'

Perhaps I shouldn't be so surprised at the level of discrimination that these 'so-called' supporters engage in. It seems to be something that is part and parcel of every football club and Ayr United is no exception. In the first half of the seventies, I was one of a group of decent youngsters who were discriminated against by almost everyone with whom we came into contact. Within the Ayr United Supporters Association in the seventies, there had been a growing intolerance of young people who got behind the team by singing songs and chanting players' names etc. We were perceived to be hooligans by the association office bearers and treated as such. It was very unlike today. I do not ever remember openly criticising players. We gave the team backing from start to finish in every game. On the supporters bus we had a great time going through our full repertoire of songs on our journeys. We never did anyone any harm but the 'decent' 'upstanding' supporters frowned upon our behaviour. You may recognise the types? They would sit in the stand and clap respectfully while showing disdain for those of us who had the temerity to make noise. Our bus convener fitted that description perfectly. In subsequent years he could be seen at the front door of Somerset Park on match days ensuring that nobody entered the players and officials entrance without authority. He was very important. At least that is what he believed. To add to our alienation, my friends and I had to endure bullying from our older colleague supporters, on the coach to away games and when we arrived in towns and cities such as Airdrie, Motherwell, Glasgow, Edinburgh and Dundee. We then had to try to avoid all the Cadbury's Fruit and Nut cases in the shape of the real hooligans of Scottish football. If we managed to escape the clutches of opposition thugs, we then had to negotiate the bus journey back to Ayr hoping that we would arrive home in one piece. It was very unpleasant at times and it was a scary period in which to be a young Ayr supporter.

We would board the Ayr United supporters coach at John Street in Ayr, just outside the building that housed the DHSS at the time and as the first people there we would obviously get to choose our seats. Four or five of us would take up the back seats only to be forced out when the bigger and older guys arrived. They would grab, punch and kick us until we finally submitted and moved out of 'their' seats. The bus convener, never batted an eyelid. I would guess the ages of Big Tam and his associates at 18 to 21 years old. They fancied themselves as hard men but in reality they were anything but. They were a cowardly bunch, adept at making our lives a misery but if anyone their own size had challenged them they would have cowered in fear. I still see a few of the very same people in the Somerset Road end to this day. They stand in their usual place, quite high on the terracing, about 10 metres to the left of the goal. They draw attention to themselves by criticising the team, hurling abuse at every opportunity and I honestly believe they relish the thought of Ayr losing as it gives them the opportunity to behave in the moronic way that they have always done. The fact that they are in their late fifties or older, suggests that there is no hope for them. The inane drivel that emanates from that area of the ground beggars belief. It's a common occurrence for spectators in the crowd to engage in imbecile watching when this lot get started. Most people laugh at them while these fools believe they are being admired. It's called self-delusion.

Two really despicable acts perpetrated by these so-called Ayr United supporters have stuck in my mind from four decades ago. In March 1970, my friend, Alex Murphy, turned up for one of our trips with a brand new jacket. It was one of these puffy, Michelin Man type jackets in royal blue. Thick and warm, it was an impressive bit of gear. Alex was a mild mannered, friendly guy who would never have done anyone any harm. Having endured the usual match day ritual of being ejected from the back seats of the bus, Alex and I sat in the row one from the back. Big mistake! Our 'friends' in the back seat noticed the jacket. Not that they said anything. We arrived in Edinburgh for a League match against Hearts, got off the bus and as Alex walked in front of me I noticed that there were several black marks across the back of the jacket from shoulder to shoulder. I told Alex and when he took the jacket off we discovered that there were five cigarette burns in a line, the jacket was ruined. We then watched our team being soundly thrashed 3-0 at Tynecastle before sharing the coach journey back to Ayr, trying to avoid physical abuse at the hands of the morons. These were our fellow Ayr United supporters.

The very same season, on our way back from Motherwell, after another 3-0 defeat, I sat quietly looking out the window, minding my own business. The bus was passing through Prestwick Toll en route to John Street when I was suddenly pulled out of my seat. I was held down on the floor of the bus by two of the gang while a third pulled off one of my shoes. He then slid open the small window that ran along the top of the main window of the bus and threw my shoe out of it. I ran to the front of the bus and shouted at the convener to stop the bus. After listening to my explanation of what had just occurred, he was particularly supportive. 'If we stop the bus and you get off, you'll be on your own, we'll be driving on,' I had no choice. I got off the bus and as it pulled away I could hear the cheers of the morons in the back seat as they waved to me, delighting in this latest victory of theirs. I eventually found my shoe and then walked the three miles home in the rain. These pathetic individuals were relentless in their bullying but the person responsible for the conduct of supporters on the bus turned a blind eye.

On the away days on which we managed to survive the ordeal of attacks from our colleague supporters, we also had to be careful on the streets of Scotland's towns and cities, before the match, inside the ground and afterwards. It was a common occurrence on away days to return home with bumps, scratches and bruises and I somehow perceived it as a social hazard that was part and parcel of being a football supporter at the time.

Mixing With The Big Boys

At no time did I feel comfortable in my new role as an apprentice painter and decorator but it was a job that provided me with an income of six pounds, three and fourpence per week and that was not to be sniffed at. A month later I was forced into learning a new financial language when, on 15 February 1971, decimalisation was introduced. My weekly wage packet now consisted of six pound notes and 17 new pence and, just like everyone else in the country; I spent an inordinate amount of time converting new money into old money in order to find out how much I was 'really' paying for things. Maybe it was my imagination but everything seemed to become more expensive overnight. I mean, McCowan's penny dainties went from one old penny to one new penny. Who could justify such a hike in price? As a new penny was worth approximately 2.4 old pennies, we're talking about a 240% price rise. My thoughts at the time were that if they were doing that with penny caramels, they must be ripping us off with everything. It took months before people finally got to grips with the new money to the extent that we stopped converting it all back to the old money every time there was a cash transaction. That six pounds and 17 new pence kept me in my painting apprenticeship for longer than I would have liked. It meant that I could afford to go to all the Ayr games, home and away. There was nothing like the feeling of anticipation that a Saturday morning brought. Sanding down doors and facings, wiping up emulsion spots and making tea became so tedious and unfulfilling however, that I made up my mind to move on. So, six months into the job, I finished my Friday shift and I went into the showroom to collect my pay packet as normal. I plucked up the courage to tell Mr Law that I wanted to hand in my one-week notice. He questioned me about my reasons for leaving and as you may expect from a 16-year-old, all I could tell him was that I did not like the job. He proceeded to give me a sermon about how lucky I was to have an apprenticeship with his company, before punishing me with instant dismissal. 'If you don't want to work here, there's no point in coming in next week. Here's your pay.' He handed me my pay packet before turning around and walking back into his office. I think I was supposed to feel bad but I was elated. I could take off my white overalls and throw them in the bin. Painting and decorating was not for me and I knew it long before my six months was up. The only problem I could think of at the time involved my lack of finances. I would need to find another job quickly or I would be subjected to more Saturday afternoons with the BBC Teleprinter for company. By the Monday morning, three days later, I had started my new job. Having arrived home after my premature retirement on the Friday, my mum slapped me across the back of my head after hearing my 'good' news and, by the time the stars had stopped spinning around my head, she had declared that I would be going with her to John Street on the Saturday morning to speak to a Careers Advisor. My mother was a woman of her word and by the Saturday afternoon she and the Careers Advisor had colluded to fix me up an interview with the manager of Saxone, the shoe shop in Ayr High Street. A 15-minute meeting with the manager, Mr Campbell and the Monday morning saw me start my new career as a shoe salesman. It just would not be realistic in the current economic climate but in those days work was plentiful and there was a choice of vacancies. Not that I had a clue about what I wanted to do with my life. I had already discovered that getting my hands dirty and carrying out dogsbody tasks on building sites and outside in cold weather was a lot less appealing than working in a shop, wearing a smart suit and helping people feel good about themselves. Searching for a size nine in a 'Clansman' brogue in the stockroom was far preferable to sanding down the turnstiles at Prestwick outdoor swimming pool with frostbite becoming more of a possibility with every passing minute. There was a down side however. Getting off on Saturdays was difficult and so I had to content myself mostly with midweek matches and reading match reports in the papers.

1971-72 started with the League Cup group stages but the euphoria of drawing both Celtic and Rangers in our four-team group soon disappeared when both teams soundly beat us, home and away. When I did manage to get a Saturday off in October though, I hit the jackpot with an away day to Airdrie to watch Ayr beating the home side 4-3. One of the greatest Ayr players ever, in my opinion, won the game almost single-handedly. To me, Johnny Graham was superb every time he pulled on an Ayr shirt. He brought a bit of class to the Ayr midfield. His ball control was excellent, he could go past players with ease and he was a prolific goalscorer. On this particular day he scored all four Ayr goals to edge it for the 'Honest Men' and I went home a very happy fan, revelling in the performance of my favourite player. I could probably name another 20 players from Ayr United teams who were 'my favourite' at one time or another. While I'll always have a soft spot for Dick Malone, Johnny Graham, in my opinion, was the cream of the crop in terms of skill.

In the same season, I also managed to get to a Scottish Cup replay against Motherwell on 1 March 1972 and it was in quite unusual circumstances. The miners strike, followed by the government announcement of a three-day working week for industry, required football clubs to play matches without the use of floodlighting, so as to conserve electricity supplies. As a consequence, the match was played on a Wednesday afternoon and that meant that I was able to travel through to Fir Park, as it was my day off. There was something exciting and yet a bit surreal about playing a blood and guts Cup tie on a Wednesday afternoon but the novelty was outweighed by the disappointment of losing a late goal to end our interest in the competition. I can still recall the incredible roar that went up from the Motherwell support when they won a corner on the left. The ball was lifted in and the next thing I knew, it was nestling in the back of the net. Gutted! All in all, it was a mediocre season for the club but a 12th place finish in the 18 club top division wasn't too bad. The following season was to get a whole lot better for several reasons. My career as a shoe salesman had lost appeal and when my dad suggested joining him in the family business, I didn't need to be asked twice. He had just taken on the lease of a fish and chip shop in Dalmilling and soon after he bought the grocers and off licence shop that sat next door to the business. I negotiated Saturday as my day off and although I worked a six-day week, it was worth it.

A sixth place finish in the First Division, a magnificent Cup run and Kilmarnock being relegated, all contributed to a memorable campaign. The shine was taken off the celebration of Killie's relegation with the realisation that there would be no League fixtures between our clubs in the following season. Nevertheless, it was amusing at the time. The final League table for the season showed Celtic, Rangers, Hibernian, Aberdeen and Dundee followed by AYR UNITED sitting proudly in sixth place. We were mixing with the big boys now. Yes, 1972-73 saw exciting times return and Ayr were giving us another season to remember. The 17th March 1973 was one of those fantastic away days for the fans, the quarter-final of the Scottish Cup against Partick Thistle at Firhill. As ever, ahead of any match I was looking for newspaper articles to find out what the journalists said about Ayr's chances. We were usually portrayed as the plucky wee team who would make a game of it but in reality they never gave us a chance. The patronising attitude of the press was never more apparent than on the night before the Thistle quarter-final. The *Evening Times* ran an article, which concluded that the four semi-finalists would be Rangers, Celtic, Dundee and Partick Thistle. The writer concluded that '…the Partick men do things just that little bit quicker'. In the *Daily Record* on the morning of the match, an article by Hugh Taylor concurred. He complimented Ayr United before going on to say about Thistle '…their pace and fervour can clinch it'. So that was a nice little pat on the head for us. Off you go now, the big teams will take it from here. Supercilious fools.

A massive crowd of Ayr fans travelled up to Glasgow by train, bus and car to take Firhill by storm. In the standing enclosure that ran along the length of the pitch, a single line of police officers separated the Thistle and Ayr fans. There was real tension in the air and 20 minutes before the start of the match, with both sets of fans hurling abuse at one another, something had to give and it did. Having paid my 15p admission, I took up my position near the front of the Ayr crowd. Looking up at the bedlam on the terracing above me, I saw a bottle thrown from the Thistle crowd, smashing against a girder up in the roof area and showering the Ayr fans below with broken glass. That seemed to signal an onslaught from the home support and seconds later, the air was filled with cans and bottles flying towards the away support. As the violence increased and police reinforcements rushed into the area to quell the unrest, I ran for my life, along with a section of the Ayr support, towards the open terraced area behind one of the goals. We watched as several Ayr supporters were helped away with a variety of minor injuries and one wee man, who I would say was in his sixties, sat on the terracing with blood pouring from a head wound. A young boy with a nasty cut above his eye and his clearly upset dad were being helped by a policeman, while a number of Partick Thistle supporters were being plucked out of the crowd by police and marched out of the ground with arms twisted up behind their backs. I have never been so scared at a football match before or since that day. There were people there who were hell-bent on causing trouble and inflicting damage on others. The scenes were ugly and I would have to say, it all came from the Partick Thistle supporters. In the *Glasgow Herald* on the following Monday morning, Ian Archer headed his column with 'Mini-Riot Ruins Expectations of a Fine Contest'.

In his report he was scathing about the type of people who engage in this type of behaviour and on this occasion, he was spot on.

I was still feeling traumatised when the game finally kicked off and after only five minutes, Partick Thistle opened the scoring. This was going to be one of those days. The Ayr supporters had been thrashed by their violent Glasgow counterparts and now the Jags players were intent on giving our team a thrashing too. Thankfully, the Ayr players had not read the script and decided that they were not going to play a bit part in this particular sporting melodrama. We were treated to a master class of football by a very talented group of Ayr players.

The very qualities attached to our opponents, by the sycophantic Glasgow press, permeated our team. Our 'pace and fervour clinched it'. We did things, 'just a little bit quicker'. In truth, we dismantled Partick Thistle with a breathtaking display of fast paced, attacking football, pinging passes across the playing surface like the top quality team we were at the time. Wee Davy McCulloch scored two goals in the first half, George 'Dandy' McLean scored two in the second half and Johnny Doyle provided the icing on the cake, to top off a magnificent performance, with a fifth. Three truly great Ayr United players got the goals. Davy McCulloch could do no wrong as far as the Ayr United faithful were concerned. I once saw Davy miss a chance at the Somerset Road end at a home match. He was three-yards from goal and somehow screwed his shot wide. He held up his arms in anguish and apology to the Ayr support and they responded by chanting his name loudly. Johnny Doyle? He brought the Somerset Road end to fever pitch as Ayr attacked in the second half of our matches. They would give him the ball at his feet on the right touchline and at that point the roar of the crowd would be deafening. We would watch the opposition defence panic as he took on one, then another and another, before putting over pinpoint crosses for the forwards or taking it on to score himself. Sadly, Johnny Doyle died in 1981 at the age of 30 after an accident at his home. He was a Celtic player at the time of his death but he will forever be remembered as an Ayr United 'Great'. As for big 'Dandy', all Ayr supporters will be forever grateful to Rangers for making the ridiculous decision to scapegoat big George for the defeat suffered by the Glasgow giants against Berwick Rangers in the Scottish Cup in 1967. When he finally found his way to Somerset Park, he still had great skill and vision and it was a pleasure watching him tease the opposition. Ayr fans at the time will remember a Rangers player being turned inside out by 'Dandy' and as he pulled the big man's shirt, big George just stopped playing and gestured to his opponent that he might like to have his jersey. What a character, what an entertainer.

Final score? Partick Thistle 1 Ayr United 5.

The bus home that evening could have made the journey without fuel. We were so ecstatic with joy, that we could have carried it back down the road.

Battling Injustice

If my journey through the seventies as an Ayr United supporter could be described as a roller-coaster, I was at the very top of the ride at this time. The feeling of anticipation ahead of a Scottish Cup semi-final against Rangers, to follow on from the Partick Thistle success, was more than any fan could ask for. It was not a dream, it was actually happening and I believed that I was the luckiest person alive to be part of it. I had to wait for another 18 days for the semi-final match and it was an excruciatingly long wait, despite a couple of wins, against Hearts and Falkirk, to keep my mind occupied. On the weekend before the tie, Ayr were up in Dundee and lost 2-1 at Dens Park but there was no doubting the team would be ready for the big Hampden event on the Wednesday evening.

The Watergate scandal in the USA was in full flow but not to be outdone, we had our very own Watergate scandal in Scotland and Ayr United were the victims. The torrential rain of 4 April 1973 was to cost Ayr United a place in their very first Scottish Cup Final but it is with a great deal of bitterness that I look back at that day. What should have been a celebration of football turned into a fiasco, depriving us of our shot at glory. At 7pm on that Wednesday evening, I was in my place on the Hampden terracing, having paid my 33p at the turnstile. I watched as half a dozen men frantically stabbed at the surface of the pitch with garden forks, trying in vain to clear the surface water so that the match could go ahead. The rain never relented and I fully expected an announcement to declare the game postponed due to an unplayable pitch. As a fanatical football fan, I hoped that the game could go ahead but on reflection, playing on a waterlogged pitch was never going to be in Ayr's interests. We were top of the ground specialists with skilful ball players. We had a team who played a fluid passing game and our opponents were the hard men of Scottish football. I still wanted the game to be played. After much deliberation and, no doubt, account being taken of the crowd of over 50,000, the teams came out and the game started. As early as the first minute of the match, it was clear to me that the decision had been a good one. A long diagonal ball was played into the Rangers penalty area and Alex Ingram rose majestically to power a header home. 1-0 to Ayr, it was going to be our night. Having reached the Scottish Cup semi-final for the first time in our history, we were now about to go one better and march on to the Final on 5 May.

The celebrations that had ensued among the Ayr support when the ball hit the back of the net were brought to an abrupt end however, when the referee signalled that Ingram had been in an offside position when the ball was crossed to him. From our position, close to the halfway line, it was impossible to tell if he had been offside or not but we were all agreed, never offside, terrible decision. As it happened, the grainy television pictures later showed that the Ayr player was indeed onside. It is an injustice that I have ranted about ever since.

Worse was to follow. We were unable to play the fast flowing, attacking football that we had become renowned for, as a passing game was impossible on a pitch covered in pools of water. The conditions were ideal for the big bruisers of Rangers. Two identical goals sealed our fate that night and while I would have accepted defeat gracefully had the opposition outplayed us, the manner in which the goals occurred was soul destroying. Four minutes before half-time, Big 'Sanny' McAnespie attempted a pass back to the Ayr 'keeper, Davie Stewart, and a puddle of water stopped the ball short. Derek Parlane nipped in to accept a gift of an opportunity and Rangers went in at the break one up. The non-appearance of Johnny Graham for the second half was a big disappointment. The Ayr star had carried an injury into the match and was unable to continue. The misery was piled on when, after 57 minutes, McAnespie was a victim once more of the puddles on the Hampden surface and Parlane was there again to make the score 2-0. Derek Parlane was a prolific goalscorer but this must have been the easiest brace of goals he would ever bag. The *Daily Record* match report the following morning was toe curling. Their version of the event in the first minute of the match typified their cosy relationship with the Old Firm: '…but there was an early shock when 'Dixie' Ingram headed past Peter McCloy in the opening minute. He was obviously offside'.

The report banged on about Rangers' superiority but the truth was that the horrendous conditions suited the big bruisers and worked against the classy, free- flowing, pass-it-on-the-deck style of Ayr United. The Glasgow press were oblivious to that fact. So, it was a 2-0 defeat by Rangers in the 1973 Scottish Cup semi-final that should never have taken place. We were robbed by the conditions and a disallowed goal by 'Dixie' Ingram in the first minute of the match, a perfectly legitimate goal.

Cup Finals and League titles are ten a penny to the big Glasgow clubs' fans but I can still feel the atmosphere of 'big' matches involving Ayr United from the time when I was just 12 years old. I have instant recall of the smallest details on days that meant so much to me and my fellow 'Honest Men'. To be fair, it has probably been more about glorious failure than great success but maybe it is not just about winning. Maybe it is about belonging and the sense of affiliation to and with my club.

The pleasure and excitement of those big matches was offset by the violence that was part of the 'beautiful' game at that time and just in case we were starting to get above ourselves we were reminded that being football fans in the seventies was not exactly one big love-in. Ahead of our groundbreaking semi-final against Rangers, we had one particularly tough away day. Dens Park, Dundee in March 1973 was the setting for an angry confrontation with 'fans' of the local club. Our supporters' buses were surrounded by an ugly mob of Dundee fans. They were ugly in mood and, coincidentally, quite ugly to look at as well. They had beaten us 2-1 but despite that fact, by the time we had started our journey back home that day, 50 per cent of the windows on our coach had been smashed. No reason was required for the spontaneous outburst of violence. It was just the done thing at the time. Smashing up the away supporters' bus was a hobby, a pastime. The police tried to disperse the crowd but they were helpless to prevent the stones being thrown at the bus from all sides. The tough guys at the back of the bus were below the seats just like the rest of us. After a discussion between the police, the bus driver and the convener the decision was made to carry on back to Ayr on the same coach, despite the new air conditioning. On other occasions we were forced to flee from groups of thugs hell-bent on doing us severe physical harm. It never took the gloss off what was a really memorable season but we had to be careful wherever we went on our travels, as we were likely to be attacked at any time.

Easter Road, Edinburgh, September 1973 and after a 4-2 defeat, I was with about a dozen Ayr fans walking back to the supporters bus when a group of green and white adorned 'supporters' attacked us from behind. Everyone in our group dispersed and, separated from the others, I ran and ran until I reached a row of shops. I ducked into a curtain shop and asked for help. A lady in the shop immediately ushered me into the back shop and reassured me that, 'they wouldn't dare come in here.' Ten minutes later she declared the coast was clear and I made my way back to where the bus was parked, relieved to have avoided a kicking. On arrival at the bus, the convener, Ian McPherson, made a speech, warning several of us that if there was any repeat of our behaviour we would be barred from the bus. '… you lot cause trouble everywhere you go,' I protested my innocence but it made no difference. Running away from unprovoked attacks was perceived to be causing trouble. So that was me on a warning.

My next major indiscretion occurred in November of the same year. We were at Firhill for a League game against Partick Thistle and as the time wound down on yet another 3-0 away defeat, my mate John and I made our way to the exit to make a quick get-away when the final whistle blew. The reason for our haste was simple. We both fancied getting a fish supper on the way back to the bus and we would have been in trouble if we delayed the journey back home. We rushed to the fish and chip shop and once served we walked at a good pace until the coach was in sight. We then relaxed, unwrapped our newspaper-covered meals and began eating in the knowledge that we would be in plenty of time. I had eaten three or four chips and had not even started on my fish when a roar came from behind us and a dozen Jags 'fans' were chasing us down the street. Both the fish suppers were cast aside, never to be eaten, as we sprinted for the safety of the bus. The commotion was heard and seen by those already on the bus and some piled out to confront our pursuers as we boarded the bus and got our breath back. We watched from the safety of the coach as the Ayr supporters grappled with their Thistle counterparts and eventually sent them packing. Our saviours returned to the bus and brought a trophy with them. They had acquired a Partick Thistle scarf from one of the mob that had chased us and two of the Ayr supporters held an end of the scarf each as they waved the new prized possession above their heads. The next 10 minutes passed without further incident and during this time the convener of the bus, who had watched the whole incident unfold, said nothing. We were waiting for the last few stragglers to get back to the bus when an older Thistle fan approached the bus shouting loudly about his son's scarf being stolen. One of the guys who had taken the scarf as a spoil of war then quickly hid the scarf under a seat. Bus convener McPherson was all of a sudden concerned. He came up the aisle of the bus and demanded the scarf and the person who had stolen it. Nobody responded and after a series of threats he gave up and went back to the door of the bus to tell the concerned father that there was no scarf on the bus. There was and he knew it because he saw the scarf being brought onto the bus and did nothing. There were plenty of us giving the father some home truths about his innocent little offspring as he stood demanding justice. Ten minutes earlier the six-footer had been focused on doing John and me some serious damage and now he was a poor victim of an unprovoked attack. The father eventually gave up his protest and walked off with his son, muttering away to himself as he pushed the taller figure of his son ahead of him. McPherson was not finished however. He came back up the aisle of the bus and demanded once again that the scarf thief own up to be dealt with by the supporters' club. One of the guys who had come to our aid put him on the spot, 'How come you saw it all happen and you were laughing when the scarf was paraded on the bus? Now all of a sudden it's disgraceful'. The convener ignored the challenge and carried on with a rant about the people responsible being found. 'I want the names of every one of you,' he said. I could not keep my mouth shut. I had remembered how I was treated after the Hibs attack and this was virtually the same thing happening again. I was incensed. I had lost my fish supper and once again I was one of the people who was being blamed for yet another crime when, in fact, we were the victims of another unprovoked attack on us. 'You can have my name if you like because I've done nothing wrong,' Another two people offered their details and the convener duly noted the names down.

I expected to hear nothing more about the incident but a few weeks later a letter arrived at my home and I was summoned to appear in front of the Ayr United Supporters Association Committee. They had managed to identify four people in total and we were all in the dock that night. The special meeting took place in the gym at Somerset Park and when I arrived the seating had been arranged with chairs for the defendants set back about three yards from the table where the six-member committee sat. The chairman was hilarious. Dressed in a charcoal grey, pin striped suit, sparkling white shirt, crimson red tie and matching handkerchief hanging out of his breast pocket, he was dressed for the occasion, our day (or evening) in court. One more feature of this splendid individual was a giant cigar held in place between his forefinger and index finger as he puffed away creating plumes of smoke and a strong unpleasant stench that permeated the whole room. The 'hearing' was an appalling affront to justice. The first person asked to speak was the convener of the bus on that day. Ian McPherson's story was a total fabrication. His submission said in effect that he had seen all of the 'accused' involved in a fight with Partick Thistle supporters and when the scarf was brought onto the bus he had demanded that he be given it straight away. None of his story was true. He had manufactured the tale to suit his agenda. He also supplemented his lies with his tall tale of previous trouble at the Hibs match. After his false account the chairman appeared to be summing up. He started spouting off about; 'this type of behaviour not being tolerated by this association blah, blah, blah' and at this point it had become apparent to me that, two minutes into this 'trial', the judge was about to hand down the sentence. I raised my hand to speak and I was given a curt, 'what is it?' Coupled with a deep frown from the chairman. 'We haven't even been asked our version of events,' I said. He let out a sigh of exasperation and shook his head as he said, 'Right, let's hear your story...for what it's worth.' That was a clear indication of how open-minded he was. He had already made up his mind and we were guilty. Letting me speak was an inconvenience and although I knew the writing was on the wall, I still wanted to have my say. I looked at all six committee members as I spoke and I recounted the events exactly as they happened. I also explained how we had been attacked after the Hibernian match and how the shopkeeper helped me. I pointed out that I had never been in trouble before and the cigar interjected, 'Not yet'. That comment made me angry and I then blotted my copybook by referring to the bus convener as a liar. That ensured that the chairman stopped me in my tracks. Still puffing on his big fat cigar, hardly appropriate for the occasion, he picked up on the sermon I had interrupted, to continue with lambasting all of us before handing down the sentence. 'You are suspended from the supporters association until further notice. You can no longer travel in the supporters' club coaches and you can no longer have any of the benefits to be derived from being members of the association. You will be sent a letter of confirmation.' The statement in itself was completely bizarre. What benefits? Travelling to away games on a rickety bus? Oh, and I once attended the annual Player of the Year dance, which incidentally was an expensive night out in the ballroom at the Darlington Hotel in Miller Road, now the home of L.A. Bowl.

What happened at that disciplinary meeting was a frustrating example of how young people at the time were discriminated against. None of the other members of the committee spoke. To be fair, some of them did nod approvingly at the chairman at various stages of his speech but there was no conference, no adjournment to consider the evidence from the hearing. Well, there would have been no evidence to consider. Nobody asked questions of me or any of the others accused of these heinous crimes. We were not represented by anyone and we certainly were not given the opportunity to question our accuser. In fact, it was never made apparent what my transgressions had been. It amounted to all of us being found guilty of 'trouble making' and in the absence of any clear cut facts of wrongdoing, the committee, or the cigar puffing chairman to be more accurate, based the decision on a skewed perception and stereotypical views of young people.

I was officially a hooligan but being suspended from the supporters association was no great hardship. I would still manage to get to games by using public transport. Nevertheless, I could not let it go. Several months later I penned a letter to the supporters association, pleading my innocence and requesting that my ban be lifted. Thirty-eight years later I am still waiting for a reply. I could have murdered a couple of people back then and I would have been back on the streets long before now. Instead, I did absolutely nothing wrong and I am still serving my sentence. That is the small-minded, power hungry people of the 1973 Ayr United Supporters Association for you.

The 1973-74 season was another good one for us as the team finished seventh in the top division. I was part of a small group of Ayr supporters who travelled by minibus to watch Ayr play Leicester City in a Texaco Cup match at Filbert Street. We had drawn 1-1 at Somerset in the first leg, where Peter Shilton showed his class as a goalkeeper, and although we lost 2-0 in the away leg, the team had given a good account of themselves and the trip was a good experience. A highlight of that season was the eagerly anticipated Scottish Cup quarter-final replay against Hearts. Ayr had held their opponents to a 1-1 draw at Tynecastle on Saturday 9 March and we had the added bonus of escaping from Gorgie without being lynched by the Hearts thugs, who had the reputation of being Scottish football's most violent supporters. Four days later, we were treated to another one of those magical nights at Somerset Park. More than 15,000 spectators piled into Ayr's ground that night and you could have cut the atmosphere with a knife. Behind the goals at the Railway End, the Ayr and Hearts fans were separated by a five-foot gap that ran from the bottom steps of the terrace right up to the back of the enclosure. My brother suggested that we take advantage of the standoff between the rival supporters to get a really good view of the pitch from the gap that was created. As the kick-off time approached, the Ayr fans continuously goaded their Edinburgh counterparts and the Hearts supporters finally snapped after an open can of beer went spinning through the air, leaking its contents as it somersaulted towards the maroon and white clad followers who filled the half of the 'shed' closer to the north terrace. The Hearts crowd surged towards their Ayr tormentors and the black and white army deserted in their droves as they hurriedly retreated towards Tryfield Place.

It could easily have turned out to be a night of catastrophe when one draws a comparison with the events of that evening and the disaster that unfolded at the Heysel stadium in Belgium where, 11 years later, 39 Juventus supporters died in a crush as they tried to escape stampeding Liverpool supporters.

We stood still in our places as the Hearts fans chased their rivals across the terracing, packing them into the corner of the ground. No Hearts supporters touched or threatened us and after the initial rush, they returned to their places. At that point, the police entered the crowd and things settled down, just in time for the kick-off.

The game itself never matched our anticipation. It wasn't exactly a classic. Johnny Doyle had been identified as the Ayr danger man and the treatment he was subjected to by the Hearts defenders was appalling. They fouled him incessantly throughout the match and the referee gave him no protection at all. After 90 minutes there had been no breakthrough. The drama that unfolded in extra-time however, had everyone on tenterhooks. I always hated the sight of Donald Ford, the Hearts centre-forward. He was a proven goalscorer and was a real threat to any defence. He was the one who opened the scoring but Ayr replied when big Rikki Fleming came up for a corner to head home the equaliser. To say that Hearts were disappointing after that would be an understatement. They sat back in their own penalty area as Ayr laid siege to their goal. Alex Ingram finally found the space to power in a header and as the Ayr crowd rose to acclaim 'Dixie' as the hero, Jim Cruikshank pulled off the save of a lifetime to deny us and keep Hearts in it. On the rare occasions that Hearts were in the Ayr half, Ford still looked dangerous and it was he who spoiled our night when he headed the winner. I could bleat all day about the fact that we outplayed them, but Hearts went through. It had been another good cup run but it ended in glorious failure…again.

The blackest day I have experienced as an Ayr United supporter came in 1975 and it was also a defining moment in my life. The stress, fear and humiliation I experienced on the last weekend of the 1974-75 season, coupled with the subsequent anger, bitterness and frustration I felt was profound and it has stayed with me ever since. It was 26 April to be precise. Thanks to a pair of unscrupulous public servants, I feel compelled to confess the fact that I was convicted of a criminal offence related to a football match on that day. The incident I speak of left me bewildered and resentful and my strong feelings on this matter have remained from that day to this. It was an important season for Ayr United, as League reconstruction was being implemented at the start of the following season. Ayr needed to finish in the top 10 of the First Division to enter the newly formed Premier League in season 1975-76. As the season drew to a close, the team were safely positioned, vying with Hearts for seventh place and that is where Ayr eventually finished the campaign, one point ahead of the Edinburgh team. The final League game of the season was away to Greenock Morton. Although there was nothing to play for in respect of the Championship or relegation, a decent crowd of about 500 travelled up from Ayr to Greenock for the match. On these occasions the atmosphere was always light-hearted and a kind of celebration of the season reaching a conclusion. I travelled up on a supporters' bus with four of my friends and we went into a social club near the ground before kick-off. We met a group of Morton supporters and shared a drink and had a good chat with them about how our teams had fared during the season and about our expectations for the following season. Morton had finished close to bottom and were already doomed to a new season in the second tier of Scottish football.

Everything about the day was normal and even when we were approached by a fellow Ayr supporter who wanted to warn us of a potential problem, we took what he said with a pinch of salt. We were walking up towards the ground when someone shouted from behind us. 'Haw guys' the voice boomed. When I looked round, I recognised the man in his thirties as someone who had travelled up to the game on our bus. 'Just watch yourselves today. I was just talking to a policeman at the corner back there. He was boasting that there will be plenty of us trying out the new police cells at the station tonight'. He continued with his cautionary tale, '…I said to him that there would be no trouble at this game today but he just laughed and said it again'. I responded by shrugging my shoulders as I certainly never saw it as a threat to any of us of being arrested.

We took our place on the terracing opposite the main stand and throughout the game there was singing and some gentle banter between both sets of supporters congregated under the enclosure. In those days there was no segregation of fans and for this game it presented no problems whatsoever. At half-time we moved our position and took up a place behind the goals that Ayr would be shooting towards in the second half. The end of the ground we were now in was open terracing, the weather was good and the group of around 200 Ayr fans who had walked around to this part of the ground were going through the full repertoire of songs and chants and generally having a good time ahead of the teams reappearing for the second half. Five of us were standing about 10 yards behind this group, higher on the terracing, giving us a good view of the pitch. The first half of the match had been uneventful and to be honest, with the second half now underway it was following the same pattern with very few goalmouth incidents. It was just a drab, end of season affair with the players perhaps looking forward to their upcoming holidays.

With about 20 minutes left, a ball was played into the Morton penalty area but a loud whistle stopped the players in their tracks. There was some confusion among players from both sides and then I noticed the referee waving 'play on'. It seemed a bit strange but it all became clear a few seconds later when two policemen jumped the small perimeter wall and went into a small group of Morton supporters who were standing close to the corner flag. One of the policemen then jumped back over the wall onto the trackside and the second officer lifted a small boy over the wall onto the track. As soon as all three were back on the pitch side of the wall, the officers took an arm each and the boy, who I guessed was around 12 years old, was marched towards the pavilion which was situated underneath the main stand. This meant that the youngster was going to be paraded in front of the Ayr supporters, on his way round the track. Curiosity about the apprehension of the boy was soon satisfied when it became clear that one of the policemen had a whistle dangling by a length of string from his free hand. The Ayr supporters in front of us instantly saw the plight of the youngster and made their opposition to the arrest of the boy clear when they entered into a chorus of, 'If you hate the Greenock Polis, clap your hands,' just as the party of three passed in front of them. It was all very light-hearted and the two policemen reflected the mood with broad smiles. The song came to a climax with, '…if you hate the Greenock polis, hate the Greenock polis, hate the Greenock polis, clap your hands'. At that point, our group of five clapped our hands three times, as is customary at the end of the chant. As things settled back down we were agreeing that it would have sufficed if the whistle had been taken from the youngster and he had been given a telling off but it seemed like his punishment was to be thrown out of the ground at the very least.

Seconds later, completely out of the blue, I felt myself falling backwards onto the terracing steps as I was dragged from behind by someone who was a good deal stronger than me. I could see the look of shock on the faces of my friends as they turned to watch me being pulled away from them by my attacker. I had already assumed that my nemesis was some Cadbury's Fruit and Nut Case, Morton supporter who had been released from the local asylum for the day and had decided to perpetrate a random assault on the first person he came across. In that split second I could not help but be confused as to why my mates were not getting him off me. When I finally did get a look at the attacker, I instantly realised why they never came to my aid. It was a policeman who had grabbed me from behind. Once he allowed me to get back to my feet, he marched me up the terracing towards one of the exits, tightly gripping my arm. All the way I was speaking to him, 'What happened?…What did I do?…Where are you taking me?…I don't understand, what's happening?' He never responded to anything I asked, never once said a word to me. As we reached the exit, one of my friends, Jim Stewart (Jazz), ran up from behind and said to the policeman, 'Why are you taking him away? He never did anything wrong'. He followed up his protest with, 'Where are you taking him?' At that point, the policeman finally broke his silence but only to say to my friend, 'Come with me and I'll show you'. He grabbed Jazz with his free hand and another policeman met him at the exit gate where he handed us both over to the control of the other officer. There was a large police van sitting at the side of the road with the back doors open. The police officer who now held us, ushered us into the back of the van where there were another two Ayr supporters, protesting their innocence and pleading to be set free. I was so shocked and traumatised by these events that I sat in silence and was close to tears. I was frightened and given that the police would do this to me when I had done nothing wrong, I was in trepidation about what they might do next. My back was hurting quite badly from my fall onto the terracing steps and my arms felt like they had been pulled out of their sockets, such was the force that had been exerted by my captor. I had not seen him coming. I did not even know he was there until I was on my back. He must have been about 6ft 2in tall and he was heavily built. As I pleaded with him for an explanation on our journey towards the police van I etched his face on my mind. I could not see his hair below his hat but I am sure that he was dark haired. He was a bit overweight with a round face, dark, bushy eyebrows and a turned down mouth. Thirty-seven years later, I can still see his face. After the police had loaded another three or four Ayr supporters into the van, we were transported to a police station and herded into a reception area.

A very courteous police officer then took us aside one at a time while two policemen stood guard over the rest of us. One guy, who looked like he was in his mid 20s, was quite hysterical and sobbed inconsolably as he sat waiting to hear his fate. It made no difference to the way he was handled. The police were totally indifferent to his protestations of innocence. Another one of the group of arrestees had a slightly different approach. As we sat waiting for our turn to be charged by the courteous officer, this young guy, about 17 years old I would say, became very aggressive and even started making physical threats against the policemen in the room. That resulted in him being handcuffed and sat back down on his seat. He quietened down after that. Everyone in that group of fans was mystified as to what offence they had committed. When it came to my turn, I tried to explain to the courteous policeman that there must be some sort of mistake. He just told me not to worry about it as it would all sort itself out. No it would not, no it did not. Once everyone had been 'processed' we were taken through some corridors that led to a block of cells. Looking at the walls, floors, doors and fittings it was obvious that this part of the building was newly built. The walls were smooth and clean finished in a light blue colour and completely untarnished. There had been no recent activity here. We were each shepherded into a separate cell that would be our own private bedroom until Monday morning.

'Haw guys, just watch yourselves today, I was just talking to a policeman at the corner back there. He was boasting that there will be plenty of us trying out the new police cells at the station tonight. I said to him that there would be no trouble at this game today. He just laughed and said it again.'

The warning we were given earlier in the day had meant nothing to me. Having said that, if I had taken the policeman's boast seriously, what could I have done to prevent this catastrophe? As I sat in that cell with a thin blue mat on the floor my only luxury, I played the events leading to my arrest over and over again in my head. My only 'crime' was clapping my hands at the end of the song that the Ayr fans were singing, much to the amusement of the policemen who had apprehended the wee whistle blowing Morton supporter. I never sang any song, I never made any gestures. I clapped my hands three times. Did the police take umbrage at the insulting song and decide to seek retribution? Well, the officers involved seemed to take the teasing of the Ayr supporters in good part. Even if they were annoyed, why didn't the police grab people from the main group who were singing? Mind you, for all I know, they maybe did take some people from that group. As I mulled things over, I mused that my fate would be insignificant in comparison to that of the initial perpetrator. Yes, the whistle blower could at this very same time be on death row awaiting lethal injection. My mind drifted back home to Ayr. 'My mum will be mortified,' 'My dad won't believe me, he'll kill me.' My concerns were on a number of levels. When will the police realise that I never did anything? Will they let us out tonight? How will I get home? Will I go to court? Will I need to get a lawyer? What happens if they send me to jail? This all may seem a little melodramatic but although I can admit to having a vivid imagination and a tendency to engage in hyperbole, I was nevertheless scared out of my wits. I slept in fits and starts all Saturday night and every time I experienced consciousness, a feeling of dread came along with it. Sunday was a long, long, day broken only by my brother arriving at the police station to find out if I was alright. The police had phoned my parents on Saturday evening to inform them that I was being held and my eldest brother, Tony, was sent through to Greenock to reassure me that a lawyer would be found and everything would be resolved. He seemed sceptical about how I managed to get myself into this mess, understandably, but after I relayed my version of events, he calmed me down and eased my concerns saying, 'By tomorrow afternoon you'll wonder what all the fuss was about'.

Ask yourself this. Would you believe a 20-year-old football supporter in this pickle? After all, why would a police officer grab someone at random and 'lift' him when he did nothing wrong? It would not happen. He must have done something. There is no smoke without fire. Although I was feeling very depressed and upset about things at this stage, I was encouraged by the knowledge that my family were now aware of what had gone on and I knew that eventually the truth would come out and I would be released with an apology. It never happened like that.

On the Monday morning, along with my friend Jazz, I was handcuffed and herded into the back of a police van before being transported to the court in another part of town. The journey took only five minutes and when we arrived we were shown into a room to meet with a court appointed lawyer. The lawyer was a dumpy little man in his fifties with a stern look and very well spoken. He was meticulously dressed in a three-piece navy blue suit and he looked over his horn-rimmed glasses when he communicated with us. He explained the courtroom procedures to us both before asking for our version of events. Annoyingly for me, he did not appear to be listening to what we were telling him. He never took notes but he waited patiently until we both ran out of steam. He then explained that he needed to establish whether we intended to plead guilty or not guilty. We were both emphatic about pleading our innocence. He replied gently, 'I advise you to plead guilty'. We both interrupted at the same time with the same reply, 'No way'. He continued, 'I know you're worried, but I want to give you the benefit of my experience so that we can end this ordeal for you. In pleading guilty, I would expect the sheriff to give you a warning, a rap on the knuckles if you like, and tell you not to do it again'. I interrupted again, 'How can I do it again if I never did anything in the first place?' Jazz added, 'All I did was ask what he did wrong, how can I be guilty?' The wee dapper lawyer continued with his 'advice' with not a trace of emotion, 'I can only advise you. The decision is up to you. I must put on record your plea before the case is called'. By this time, I had decided to take no more, 'My family are organising a lawyer for me so I don't want you to do anything'. His reply was spontaneous, 'There is no other lawyer here for you. If you both agree to plead guilty, I can approach the prosecuting lawyer and ask for the swear words to be dropped as evidence,' he said. 'What swear words?' we both blurted out at the same time. We both reminded him that we had done nothing wrong and we would not plead guilty. He had kept his powder dry, however, and his next statement obliterated our resolve. 'You've made up your minds boys. I will enter pleads of not guilty for both of you but I must warn you that the trial that follows may not be for another three or even six months'. 'Will that be here?' my mate asked. 'Yes, it will. The sheriff will set a date and you will be told whether or not you will be remanded in custody until the trial'. I asked him to repeat his last statement. 'Yes, you heard right…' he said '…you may be kept in the cells until the trial.' Well, if ever my mind was made up about how I was pleading, it was right there and then. We both submitted and agreed to plead guilty before asking him if he would see that the swearing was dropped from the charge, as he had suggested. He agreed to do that. 'I won't come back down. I'll see you upstairs in court'. As he left the room I heard myself saying 'thank you'.

Looking back now, I realise that this little man was only interested in getting through his day without any complication or fuss. He was indifferent to the fact that we were totally innocent. What a waste of an education. This man spent seven years hard graft getting to an esteemed position as a member of the legal faculty and instead of practising in an idealistic manner and trying to make a positive contribution to the justice system, he advises innocent clients to plead guilty. For what? An easy life? That day may not have been a big deal to the wee lawyer but the fallout from that weekend has stayed with me for 37 years…and counting.

'I know you're worried, but I want to give you the benefit of my experience so that we can end this ordeal for you. In pleading guilty, I would expect the sheriff to give you a warning, a rap on the knuckles if you like, and tell you not to do it again'

'I must warn you that the trial that follows may not be for another three or even six months…you may be kept in the cells until the trial'.

Of course, my mindset at that stage was entirely different from today.

My friend and I agreed that we had done the right thing. We were not worldly wise, so we needed to take a lead from the only person who was in a position to help us. Our decision was made. Although it grated with me, the important thing was to get out of the mess I was in and this *gentleman* was helping me do that. I could not have been more wrong.

We waited for another 15 minutes or so before a policeman came in and took us to another room. He explained that someone would come and escort us into court when our case came up. There was one other guy in the room. He looked about 19 or 20 years old. Although he was dressed in a suit, he still managed to look quite scruffy. His tie was askew and he was very nervous, even more scared than me. He asked me what I was 'up' for and after explaining I returned the question. He told me that he was accused of carnal knowledge of a 14-year-old. Not wanting to appear ignorant, I answered, 'ah, right'. I had absolutely no idea what he was talking about. Another 20 minutes passed before a police officer came into the room and told me and my friend to follow him. We were taken through a set of double doors and up a narrow staircase. When we arrived at the top of the staircase, I was startled to find that we were right in the heart of the court. We were in an enclosure, the dock. My stomach was churning and my palms were moist with sweat. The sheriff mumbled something incoherent before a lawyer to my left stood up and after asking us to confirm our names and addresses; he gave a summary of the charges. In among his elaborate speech I heard 'breach of the peace'. Our own little Perry Mason then stood up and declared that we were pleading guilty to the charges. A call then went out for a witness and the policeman who apprehended me, and started the ball rolling on this whole fiasco, walked into the court and took up his position in the witness box. The man who had earlier set the scene and summarised the charges stood up again and after the policeman was sworn in he asked him to give his version of events. What followed was a complete fabrication of events. His statement bore absolutely no resemblance to what actually happened. He read from a pocket book he had in his hand. Referring to me, he said, 'The accused turned to face me in my position above a group of spectators on the terraced area. The accused then challenged me to fight with him by shouting "Come on you bastard, I'll take you and all of the polis on. Fuck the lot of you…" I could not take any more of the lies and I raised my hand and said, 'Excuse me'. The interruption brought the sheriff to life. He motioned to the policeman to wait and then he addressed me. 'When you are in my court, you will not speak unless you are asked to do so'. I blurted out, 'But this is all lies'. The sheriff continued, 'If you say one more thing you will be in contempt'. I hadn't a clue what he was talking about but I realised that I was in serious trouble if I spoke again, so I stayed silent for the rest of the hearing. The policeman continued '…the accused continued shouting abuse at me and I therefore approached and took hold of the accused and held him until a colleague assisted me in restraining him'. I have often been teased by people who know me because I do not use bad language and that has not changed over the years. At no time during the events of that weekend did I use a swear word. The very notion that I challenged a policeman to fight is laughable. Yet this officer of the law chose to lie so that he could strengthen his case to ensure that I was convicted of a breach of the peace. To this day I still do not understand why he did that. Anyway, a similar statement was read out to my friend and we both looked at one another in disbelief. Once the policeman was dismissed it was our lawyer's turn again. He rambled on about his clients apologising for wasting the time of the police and the court with their foolish behaviour and that we were full of remorse blah, blah, blah. The sheriff then closed the proceedings by giving us a short sermon. 'I want to make it clear to both of you that Greenock is a nice place and we don't want your kind around here. Should your team return here, stay at home. If you appear before me again, your sentence will be severe…' It seemed like an afterthought when he added '…fined £60'. I don't want to be picky here but, '…Greenock is a nice place'? I'm not sure that anyone who makes that assertion is a fit and proper person to preside over court proceedings. He was maybe suffering from temporary delusion. I'll tell you this…it was a really nice place to get out of.

Over the course of that weekend, I had been truly shafted by a lying policeman and a lying lawyer. I would pay good money to meet up with that pair of scumbags. Not to vent my frustration in an aggressive way but to confront them and force them to explain to me why they concocted those lies about me. What self-respecting policeman would try to have a false conviction pinned on a 20-year-old who had done him no harm? Is a lawyer's work so stressful that he would compromise his integrity so that the court process would run more smoothly for him? The idea that two youngsters charged with breach of the peace would be held for up to six months on remand is utterly preposterous. Try telling that to a 20-year-old who has no knowledge of the process of law. I believed everything this despicable little man said to me. Sixty quid! That was a lot of money in 1974 and where was I going to get it? I had no idea. As it happens, I was given time to pay at a rate of £5 per month but my dad paid the full amount within a week, after he had calmed down.

My mother was anything but calm and knowing when her son is telling the truth, she decided that we should take things further. She made an appointment to see the Ayr Conservative MP George Younger and a few days later we both went along to see him at his Wellington Square office. He listened intently to everything I told him, taking notes and asking me to clarify details. I had this fanciful idea that something could still be done to right this wrong. It was my turn to be delusional. I was confident that Mr Younger would get the conviction overturned. As soon as he started speaking I realised that, no matter the pressures I had been exposed to, by pleading guilty I had given up any chance of redemption. He explained that he could do nothing about the conviction but he was very concerned about the behaviour of the lawyer who was appointed to represent us. Incidentally, the solicitor my family contacted could not arrange for anyone to be at the court on the Monday morning because of the short notice and that is why I was left with the court appointed lawyer. Mr Younger said that he would be writing to the Law Society for Scotland to inform them of my complaint. In the circumstances I felt that the MP was serious about helping and if a reprimand for the lawyer was all I could achieve, at least it was something. Mr Younger never did get back in touch, despite several follow up phone calls from my mother. My resistance petered out and I just decided to put up with the injustice. Of course, other than my family, nobody got to hear the true story of what happened on that weekend. The rest of the community only knew about the hooligan element of our family, me. The sense of shame and embarrassment was not balanced in any way by the fact that I had not done anything wrong. The *Ayrshire Post* headline read, 'Ayr Fans Pay The Price Of Trouble' and listed the 'culprits' and the fines handed out. I never spoke at length with any of the other Ayr fans who experienced the same fate as me but I would not be surprised to learn that they had a story of injustice to tell. The use of the word catastrophe does not overstate how I viewed the whole affair. At that point in my life, to be in this situation was devastating. I spent a long time with my head down, scared to look people in the eye. I assumed that people would regard me with disdain. I was lucky in one sense though. I worked in the family business. If I had been employed anywhere else I may have lost my job and how would I have found another job? Who would take on a football hooligan? Of course, that's of no concern to the liars who concocted their stories for their own ends and caused all this grief.

Knockout Football

As anyone would expect, I was keeping a low profile as the 1975-76 season started. I was genuinely fearful when I went to any of Ayr's matches, scared that I would be arrested for an imaginary crime. By the time the home League match against Rangers, in October 1975, had arrived, I was paranoid. I had decided to watch the match from the enclosure in front of the main stand and I took up my place behind the home dugout. The people around me were mainly Ayr United fans but there were a few Rangers supporters around too. As the teams ran out onto the pitch and the roar of 20,000 spectators finally subsided, a tall man in a black overcoat was shouting loudly to anyone who would listen. 'Errs a tenner says Rangers to win and I'll give ye a goal eh a start Err (Ayr).' He was waving a £10 note above his head and daring someone to take him up on his offer. 'Whits wrang we ye, dae ye no fancy yer team?' He continued to repeat his offer over and over but he received no encouragement from anyone within earshot. He had everyone turning to watch him as he ranted on with his mantra but nobody responded. The self-assurance he possessed undermined my own confidence and I started to think that Ayr would lose convincingly if he was so sure that he would risk £10. He was obviously certain that Rangers would win and he was prepared to take the risk.

Ayr started brightly and, as was usual at Somerset, they took the game to their opponents. A wonderful opening goal from Davy McCulloch sent the Ayr supporters around the ground into raptures. As soon as the game restarted, the man in the overcoat was at it again. 'Errs yer team scored a goal. That's you got two goals now. Who wants to take ma tenner?' A man standing close to me piped up, 'Put your money back in yer pocket pal, yer team's gettin' beat'. The gambler's response was swift. 'Don't worry about me, this is easy money for ye if ye believe in yer team'. The Ayr supporter decided to hold his tongue. He was not sure enough that he was prepared to risk such a large amount of money on the outcome. The game had barely restarted when Alex Ingram scored the second goal. Ayr were on fire and Rangers already looked like a beaten team. As the spontaneous celebrations subsided, there must have been about a dozen people who were shouting, 'I'll take your tenner', 'Your bet's on now mate', and other similar remarks. I looked round to where the man had been standing earlier but he had disappeared. Johnny Graham made the score 3-0 as Ayr went on to record a comprehensive victory over the Glasgow giants and I experienced that nice warm feeling that I always got from an Ayr United win. Ayr 'keeper Hugh Sproat had somehow managed to limp his way through most of that match with an injury that he picked up early on and Alex Ingram bled for the team, after a nasty leg gash that needed several stitches after the match. Hugh Sproat was a very popular character and an excellent goalkeeper for the club. He may not have been the tallest but his agility and timing were superb. Having grown up in Hayhill at the same time as Hugh, I can also testify to his all round ability as a football player. He could have been a circus act with his ball control, keepy-uppy and heading skill. The guy was a natural. His antics when the Old Firm came to town were hysterical. He wore green outfits for the visit of Rangers and Blue when Celtic came to town. His banter with the crowd was always well received and his contribution to the Ayr United cause was very much appreciated. No matter how much he accomplished as a player, he never became a 'Billy Big Boots'. He always acknowledged me in the street and still does. He is definitely one of the good guys. The headline in Saturday's edition of the *Evening Times* shouted 'RANGERS STUNNED BY AYR

DOUBLE', in reference to the two goals inside a minute. The horrible gut feeling that accompanied my weekend in Greenock would never disappear completely but this win certainly lifted my spirits.

Of the three seasons that Ayr United competed in the Scottish Premier League, this was their most successful. A sixth place finish led me, and people like me, to believe that we were one of the big guns of Scottish football. There was an expectation that we would compete at the highest level for the foreseeable future. Not only were we holding our own against the best teams in Scotland but we were also taking on big English clubs in the Anglo-Scottish Cup competition. One of these two-legged ties took place in October and November 1976 against Nottingham Forest. We had reached the semi-final stage and I was determined to get to the away match in Nottingham. In an adventurous frame of mind, and a commitment to the Ayr United cause, my friend Billy Murray and I set off for the away leg on foot. We figured that we could hitch hike our way to Nottingham and back, a 600 mile round trip. We got a lift to New Cumnock on the evening before the match and thanks to the consideration of a few car drivers and truck drivers we made it there and back, unscathed and the better for our experience. Although our journey was relatively uneventful, we did have one quite alarming experience early on. After my Greenock experience, I may still have been in a sceptical or even cynical frame of mind in regard to the integrity of police officers but I need not have worried. When we found ourselves on the side of the road just outside New Cumnock in pitch darkness, a car came round the corner and we stretched out our arms with upturned thumbs hoping for our first success at hitchhiking. As the car pulled level with us, it slowed down and the blue and red lights on top of the car burst into life. It appeared that our journey may be over before it was really started when the officers asked us to sit in the back of their car. They then questioned us about where we were going and why we were walking. Once we had explained that we were Ayr supporters travelling to Nottingham, they offered to take us down as far as Thornhill from where we would need to make our own arrangements. When they dropped us off, 20-odd miles later, they even apologised for not taking us any further.

Having managed to safely negotiate our 300 mile passage, we were finally in the City Ground, Nottingham, ready for the action. On a cold but dry October evening, this was a massive tie for us against a top English side, managed by the indomitable Brian Clough but only 50 or 60 Ayr fans had made the trip. The first 20 minutes were all about Forest holding out against a rampant Ayr attack. Malky Robertson, on Ayr's left wing, was giving the home defence a torrid time and both he and Alex Ingram came close to giving Ayr the lead. Andy Geoghegan, affectionately known as 'Gied Away a Goal Again', had virtually nothing to do in that opening period but as fate would have it, Larry Lloyd opened the scoring for Forest against the run of play on the 20 minute mark and a dominant Ayr side were now 1-0 down. From that point the game was evenly contested. I was pleased when Martin O'Neill, the now Sunderland manager, was substituted because he always looked a danger but big Peter Withe scored a second for Forest in the 75th minute and it left Ayr rueing the missed opportunities of their period in ascendancy. All was not lost however and when Johnny Graham scored from a penalty right at the death, we left the stadium hopeful about our chances in the return leg at Somerset.

I turned up for the home tie full of confidence that we could progress to the Final. My positivity was based on what had been an excellent display from Ayr at The City Ground and we were only one goal down but this game was entirely different. Somerset Park was bathed in torrential rain and Ayr were washed away by a ruthless display from Nottingham Forest. Peter Withe scored after 10 minutes and from that point Ayr were never really in it. The English team had identified Malky Robertson as the danger man and the Ayr winger was subjected to 45 minutes of disgraceful fouls to prevent his forages into the Forest half. Robertson was eventually carried off just before half-time and the lacklustre Ayr performance in the first half was repeated in the second period. Tony Woodcock scored the second for Forest to make the aggregate score 4-1 and to be fair to Nottingham Forest, they proved to be a class above our team. They went on to beat Leyton Orient 5-1 in the Final.

All things considered, it had been a good season for Ayr United and on another positive note, I had resumed my playing career, albeit five-a-side football with my brother and my mates on a weekly basis at the Magnum Centre in Irvine and in the Dam Park Hall in Ayr. My brother, Tony, formed a team for the weekly league in the Irvine sports centre and we also played in the Monday night leagues and Christmas and Easter Fives tournaments organised by Johnny Hubbard, the ex-Rangers 'Penalty King'. Enthusiastic teams from all over Ayrshire entered these seasonal competitions and converged on Dam Park during the holiday periods for wall-to-wall competition, vying with other teams to qualify from the group stages to the knockout, with extra-time and penalties to eventually decide who would win the trophy and the glory. I recovered my passion for playing during this period and our team did quite well in the tournaments, eventually winning it one year.

It was at the Dam Park Hall in Ayr in October 1977, that I sustained one of the more serious injuries of my playing career. We were involved in a match against a team that included Davy Agnew. Davy was a decent player who went on to play junior football in the years ahead. On the night in question, Alan Lawrence, a teammate of mine, had been criticising me about drawing out of tackles and during this match he was once again telling me to get stuck in. I decided to do just that and my opportunity to show that I was up to the job arrived in the shape of Davy Agnew coming towards me with the ball. He let the ball drift away from his foot and I went in hard to win the ball. I got the ball but also caught his ankle and the referee blew for a free kick against me. Although it was unintentional, Davy never saw it that way and he lunged towards me with his fists flying. I managed to grab his arms to prevent him from landing with one of his flailing fists and although I prevented him from punching me, he somehow managed to rip my strips in the ensuing struggle. He calmed down and we played out the rest of the match without further incident.

Being a talker and certainly not a fighter, I decided to go over to Davy after the game to smooth things over. Big mistake! I approached him from behind and opened up with 'Davy, what was all that about?' Davy was not in the mood for talking and in one movement he spun around towards me and sent me crashing to the floor with a knock-out punch. Apparently I came to and even played another match before someone insisted on taking me to hospital. I have no recollection of playing after the incident. I was admitted to a ward suffering from concussion and three of my front teeth had been pushed back inside my mouth. When I finally got the chance to see the damage, I realised that I was probably going to lose these teeth. I was in hospital for four days and during that time, fortunately, I had an operation that saved my teeth. The day of my operation was a very important one. The national football team were in Liverpool for a World Cup qualifying match against Wales, which they won 2-0 to qualify for the 1978 World Cup Finals, with Ally MacLeod as manager. I managed to miss the match because I had not recovered from the effects of the anaesthetic. I had to wear splints around my upper teeth for three months while things gradually settled back into place but eventually I made a full recovery and those teeth are still intact to this day. The process was a painful one and I can tell you that Davy was not my favourite person for a while. But these things happen in the heat of the moment.

Enemies and Friends

It was during the period we were frequenting Dam Park football tournaments that we became friendly with another bunch of guys who had formed a team there. Both our groups agreed to join together and we established a team to enter into the Ayrshire Amateur League. After successfully applying for registration to the league for the 1978-79 season, we dropped out of the Magnum five-a-side league and concentrated on our full-sided matches. Our first season in amateur football coincided with Ayr United's first season back in Division One of the Scottish Football League. The 'Honest Men' had finished second bottom of the Premier League in 1977-78 and were relegated along with Clydebank. Regrettably, they have never been back in the top flight since. I saw very little of Ayr United for the next few seasons as I was totally committed to my amateur team. Apparently, I never missed much as it was a particularly inauspicious time for the club. Although we concentrated on our Saturday afternoon football, we did faithfully return to Dam Park Hall for every seasonal fives tournament but our main focus was on our amateur games. We had chosen the name Kyle Thistle for the simple reason that all of our players met up in the Kyle Tavern in Kyle Street in Ayr for meetings and to have a drink. The pub sponsored us and we held our fundraising events there on a regular basis. For one of these fundraisers I contacted Pascall Murray, the confectionery manufacturers, to ask for some free samples of the pink and white gooey marshmallows to use in a sponsored competition. The company had been taken over by Cadburys in 1964 but still used the Pascall Murray name. A few days later, 12 boxes of the sweets were delivered to my home, free of charge, and I duly organised a sponsored marshmallow-eating competition. We had a full house for the mad event in the Kyle Tavern and raised over £200. The first prize, a bottle of whisky, went to Ian Queen for devouring 40 marshmallows in six minutes 45 seconds and not to be outdone, Rab Alexander ate the most marshmallows, 75 in total. I think it's safe to say that Ian and Rab were unable to look at the fluffy, pink and white cushions for quite some time after that. We followed up the event with a sausage-eating fundraiser and if my memory serves me well Ian Queen was to the fore in that competition too. There were lots of other madcap events that added to the coffers while allowing us some fun at the same time.

For the next four years, what started off as five guys having a kick about, turned into a well-organised club where we all got on like a house on fire. We had a great time on and off the park and although we were not particularly good, we enjoyed our football, win or lose. It was during this time that I came into my own and played my best football. The missing ingredient from my younger years in football was confidence and with my new found belief I developed into a…well, a very ordinary player who managed to get a game in the team along with other friends including Alan Noble, Davy Sargent, Alan Lawrence, 'Nat' Coughtrie and Billy Murray. We were all distinctly mediocre but we loved our football. After a couple of years our coach, John Stevenson, moved on and I took over the management of the team. I have always been an organiser and I enjoyed running the team as well as playing. Although we never set the heather on fire with our results, we had some stick-out players. Our mental goalkeeper, Tommy Wilson or 'Wilpy' to his teammates, could have been superb but his off the wall antics cost us dearly a lot of the time. We had talented players such as Colin Dodds and Davy Gillan and a few of our team went on to play junior football including Jimmy Nimmo, George Lyon and 'Teddy' Cole. Jimmy was a stick out for our team and I was so impressed by him that in 1980 I wrote letters to Willie McLean, the Ayr United manager and Ally McLeod, who at the time was manager at Motherwell. I pointed out to them that we had a player who should be considered for senior football. Jimmy played sweeper for us but he could have played in any position. He was certainly too good for our level. I never received any response to my letters but my point was proved, albeit three years later, when Jimmy was invited to Somerset Park for a trial with Ayr United. I went to watch the reserve match he played in and he was given an attacking midfield role. He set up two goals, hit a shot off the post and generally played well. Apparently, George Caldwell, the Ayr manager, could not see the potential I had identified. Jimmy continued in junior football and went on to play for Auchinleck Talbot at one point, so I still felt vindicated.

Like any other team, we played a number of pre-season friendly matches to prepare for the league campaign ahead and a good example of some camaraderie we had with other teams was when a team from Dennistoun in Glasgow contacted the *Ayr Advertiser* ahead of the 1979-80 season. They were looking for a team to play home and away to sharpen up for the season ahead. My brother Tony, who was the advertising manager for the paper at that time, let me know about it and after a phone call we agreed to play the Glasgow team, home and away. They came down to play us at King George V in Ayr and we had one of our good days, winning the match 7-1. We presented the Glasgow team with a shield to commemorate our match and they returned the compliment by giving each of our players a small trophy to mark our trip to Glasgow for our 'friendship' match. They were a really nice bunch of guys. On the evening of the first match we took the Dennistoun team for a night out in Ayr and we all got on like a house on fire. Two weeks later we fought out a 2-2 draw on a red blaise pitch at Glasgow Green and the Dennistoun lads returned the favour of a night out in Glasgow. A great time was had by all.

My propensity for larking around, winding people up and having too much to say for myself has got me into trouble too many times. I have always resisted the urge to take things too seriously and although I possess a very competitive streak and a burning desire to win, I have always had a light-hearted or even flippant side at times. So while on one hand I would be busting a gut, trying my best for the team, the temptation to complement my efforts with some practical jokes and childish humour was too strong a pull. However, I can say in all honesty that I have never meant anyone any harm. Most people realise this but on the odd occasion I have bitten off more than I could chew. One incident that I can recall vividly was near the end of my amateur days. Kyle Thistle had an away match in the Ayrshire Amateur League against Tarbolton Amateurs and as usual we travelled up to the village in our small convoy of cars, raring to go and in good spirits. We went ahead early on in the game when I was brought down inside the box and 'Teddy' Cole slotted home the resultant penalty kick. Our opposition were not particularly sympathetic as I limped away with a nasty swelling on my knee, evidence that the award was justified. The Tarbolton players were not in agreement with the referee and they proceeded to call me a variety of names related to my proficiency in diving. That was the signal to start my torment of my enemies. Behind the back of the referee, I put the palms of my hands together and pretended to be diving into an imaginary swimming pool on the pitch. As you can imagine, this turned me into public enemy number one and as the game restarted I was subjected to some hefty tackles complemented by verbal abuse. I just moved the teasing up a notch, a wee comment here and there, riling them, drawing fouls and getting free kicks. I had done this so many times in the past that it became second nature to me.

However, on this particular day in Tarbolton, I went too far. I was being tracked by a big left-sided midfielder who was hell-bent on kicking me at every opportunity. I would estimate his height as 5ft 10in and he was carrying a lot of weight. I was goading him about his lack of mobility throughout the first half. As we retired at half-time I heard him comment to one of his teammates, 'See that wee number eight, am gonnae break his legs in the second half'. Sure enough, as soon as the second half was underway he personally threatened me with the same promise. It was not as if I had not heard this type of threat before and being me with my annoying ways, I fired back an instant reply, 'If you want to catch me you better get yourself a motorbike big man'. The big guy was mad and made a bee-line towards me with the express intention of throttling me. I dodged away from him and teased him a bit more, 'Was that it…you should try breaking into a run'. This time I never moved quickly enough and he managed to grab my strips before I pulled away. The referee had turned towards us just in time to see him with a handful of my red and white striped top and he duly blew his whistle. He beckoned the big bear towards him and yellow carded him. The big fellow was now incensed and on his return to take up his position as my shadow he said quietly, 'I'll get you sooner or later'. I was having a great time until suddenly the tide turned. The Tarbolton captain had been observing the drama unfolding in front of him and he had decided to take an active part. He called the big guy over and instructed him to change positions with him. As the captain took up his new midfield position and sidled up to me, the guy he replaced shouted over to him, 'If you don't get him, I'll be getting him later Budgie'. 'Budgie' stood about two inches taller than me at five foot eight and I was looking up at him when he said in a calm, quiet voice, 'I'm gonnae deal wi' you now. Think you're a funny man eh…you'll be going to hospital just shortly.' I should have known better than to keep talking but I then made things worse by saying, 'You know what's wrong with you Budgie?…you've been reading too many Superman comics'. I never detected any anger in his voice as he replied in a confident, assured tone. 'You're the wan that's gonnae be fleein' through the air wee man'. I had met my match. This one had as quick a wit as me. He may have been slimmer, faster and smaller than the big guy but he was scarier too. Suddenly, I wasn't finding things quite so amusing. He could run for a start. He also had a very powerful shot with his right foot. I can testify to that because I felt the dull thud of his kick up my backside shortly after our introduction. I was sent flying several times as he exacted revenge for tormenting his mate. My game finished prematurely. I received a pass inside the centre circle and as I carried the ball forward my nemesis came flying in with both feet off the ground and he caught me on my right thigh. The tackle was the signal for a wrestling match involving half the players on the field and after the warring parties had been separated, and the handbags returned to their rightful owners, I was helped from the field as the Tarbolton captain was booked. The tackle was a nailed on red card offence if ever I saw, or felt one. Yellow, decided the referee. Considering I had started all the trouble, I probably deserved what I got. It was only after the match that I discovered the big guy was Budgie's brother and he was taking care of family business.

As the players trooped into the dressing room after the match, that incidentally finished 1-0, I was nursing my badly bruised leg and suffering from the after effects of my personal humiliation at the hands of the enforcer. The players brought with them news of a further concern for me. The Tarbolton captain had apparently informed them that he wasn't finished dealing with me. He asked my teammates to pass on the message that he would be waiting outside the dressing room for me. Now I was in a right pickle. With a lot of effort I managed to get showered and dressed, and taking a deep breath I hobbled outside to confront my fate. There he was, barring my route to the car and my so-called mates were all three steps behind me. It was obvious to me that I was getting no support from that lot. I had a decision to make. I could not make a run for it as he had already crippled me with that final thigh high challenge. I could either take my beating or plead for clemency. The latter seemed to be the most attractive option but as I started blurting out my apologies he ran towards me. Fearing the worst, I steeled myself against the inevitable impact of the punches and kicks about to rain down on me. Instead, what happened was that everyone fell about laughing as the Tarbolton captain put his arm around my shoulder and used his free hand to ruffle my hair. He had planned the whole after-match confrontation and all the Kyle Thistle players were in on it. The tables had been turned on me and I was getting my comeuppance. Comments from both sides were flying around, 'You should have seen your face, you were shitin' it'. 'Gie's another wind up wee man'. 'No sae clever noo, ur ye'? The psychological damage was one thing but my leg felt like it would never be the same again. 'Sorry about the leg wee man, you awright?' 'I can't complain, I deserved it,' I replied.

Glorious Failure

During my spell with Kyle Thistle, we had the most fun on our travels and like every other team we loved the cup matches away from home. In our third season, we had improved quite well as a team but we were prone to the odd lapse of form resulting in a thrashing. Our Ayrshire Cup hopes were shattered early on in that season with a 7-0 defeat to Ardrossan Castle Rovers but on the plus side we received a bye to the second round of the Scottish Cup. When the draw was finally made, I discovered that we were to play away against Coatbridge CC. I looked up the results from the first round of the Scottish Cup and I was a little alarmed when I read Ardrossan Castle Rovers 0 Coatbridge CC 7. It was not looking good. In our usual show of bravado we displayed our cavalier attitude and went up to Coatbridge prepared to give it a go. The initial signs never instilled us with confidence. Our opponents took to the field of play dressed in all black and every one of them was an athlete. Our strips at Kyle Thistle were red and white striped tops, which coincidentally was the same as the colours of Alloway Boys Club years earlier and identical to the strips used by Valspar

Boys Club in the years ahead of me as a coach. The Coatbridge CC coach who carried a rack of water bottles over to his touchline position looked somewhat familiar and as he then walked over to shake my hand I realised it was Alfie Conn, who had played with both Celtic and Rangers in a very successful career. I thought to myself, 'If only the bus had broken down'.

It would be true to say that the odds were stacked against us. In our plan we did not exactly envisage a win or even a draw. We would have been happy to avoid humiliation. Although we started the game quite strongly, Coatbridge soon had us pinned back and they opened the scoring after 15 minutes with an excellent move culminating in their main striker shooting home from the edge of the box. That goal was probably the best thing that could have happened to us. The home team seemed to take their collective foot off the gas and we began to enjoy more of the possession. With about five minutes left before half-time, we won a corner on the right and I went across to take it. In training, Jimmy Nimmo was always banging on about late movement at corners and winning the ball at the near post. He gestured to his head as he shouted to me, 'think about what we're doing here'. I knew he meant the near post ball for his head. Jimmy took up a central position on the edge of the penalty area but he was being shadowed closely by his marker. Big George Lyon came up from the back and made his way to the far post with two home defenders following his every step. When the referee gave the signal, I played the ball with pace at head height, level with the six-yard box. Jimmy Nimmo had timed his run with precision and managed to shake off his marker. He dived full length to power his header into the roof of the net for the equaliser with the goalkeeper flailing at the net-bound ball. After weeks of nagging us all about his near post, late run theory, Jimmy let us all know during our celebration how right he had been and he added in some terms of endearment, specially for me. 'Yesssss, ya wee fenian bastard, ye did it,' It was not sectarian, it was not discriminatory, it was very much tongue in cheek and quite amusing. It is not what is said, it's the way it is meant. There we were, wee Kyle Thistle from the Ayrshire Amateur South Third Division, still in it, holding a team who fancied their chances of going all the way to the Final. Half-time came and went and the Coatbridge team imposed themselves on the game as the second half progressed. Nevertheless, I was probably beginning to believe that there might be a possibility of taking our opponents to a replay. The thought soon disappeared after Coatbridge rattled us with two goals in three minutes.

If anything, this relaxed us and we started to create a few chances on the break. 'Teddy' Cole went on one of his runs, leaving three opponents in his wake before placing his shot well out of the goalkeeper's reach. At 3-2, and with 10 minutes left to play, we actually had a couple of chances to level things. I managed to beat the 'keeper with a free kick that came back off the bar and every time 'Teddy' Cole or Jimmy Nimmo got the ball there was panic in the home defence. At this stage the Coatbridge CC players were arguing with one another and their team was in disarray. Unfortunately, we were unable to capitalise. The game finished 3-2 and we were out of the cup but we had given a really good account of ourselves. We laughed and joked all the way to the dressing rooms with the Coatbridge CC players dumbfounded at our upbeat attitude. 'Teddy' Cole, forever the wind up merchant, cranked it up a bit as he shouted over to the home players, 'Cheer up boys, you won'. I think it was a show of defiance and pride in our performance as well as relief that the match had not turned out to be a total embarrassment.

I spent four years playing amateur football and managing Kyle Thistle before having to resign because of a new job that included Saturday working but I will always look back fondly at that time. Ahead of my new career move was yet another Ayr United highlight. Despite the failure to win a place back in the Premier League, the 1980 Bell's Scottish League Cup campaign had been going well. Ayr had disposed of Morton and Queen of the South before destroying Hearts 4-0 in a second-leg tie at Somerset, having already beaten them 3-2 in the first leg at Tynecastle three weeks earlier. My activity as an Ayr supporter at the time may have been severely rationed but the flame was re-ignited with the thrashing handed out to Hearts that Wednesday evening. Ask any Ayr fan about the atmosphere in Somerset Park that night and you will encounter superlatives by the dozen. It was like a return to the 'old days' with Ayr firing on all cylinders and the support lapping it up.

The first leg match ended in a creditable 3-2 win at Tynecastle and it set things up perfectly for the second leg and another of those fantastic cup ties under floodlights at a packed Somerset Park. The one goal advantage for Ayr at kick-off time was increased to a five goal gap by the end of the match. Bobby Connor had continued a recent goalscoring spree when he turned in a Gerry Christie cross in 16 minutes and with only six minutes left it looked like Ayr would ease to a 1-0 win and a 4-2 aggregate victory.

Now, for people with a propensity for leaving football matches early, that night was a good example of why you should always stay to the end. We certainly got our money's worth in those last six minutes. An own goal, a diving header from Derek Frye and an Eric Morris strike, after a great cross from Stevie Nicol kept us in our places long after the teams had left the field of play, singing the praises of our team.

AYR UNITED 4 - HEARTS 0 (Agg. 7-2)

Ayr were then paired with Hibs in the quarter-final and it was a chance to take revenge for our Scottish Cup exit earlier in the year. That fourth round Scottish Cup tie in February had attracted a big Ayr support to Edinburgh, not least because of the inclusion of George Best in the Hibs line-up but there was to be disappointment both at the result and the non-appearance of the Irish genius. The biggest disappointment was the 2-0 defeat but the absence of Best made an interesting story. The night before the Cup tie he had apparently bumped into the French international rugby squad, who were in town for a match against Scotland, and Jean Pierre Rives, the French captain, insisted he join the party for a drink. Best was still at the bar the next morning barely able to stand.

In this, our latest clash with Hibernian, I felt that we had let it slip in the first leg when Hibs managed to sneak a 2-2 draw. The date we played that match at Somerset Park, in the first leg, 8 October, was a familiar one. It had been that very date in 1969 when Ayr had instilled in me, great expectations of future glory in that thrilling League Cup semi-final 3-3 draw with Celtic. The feeling of déjà vu was to wash over me. When Derek Frye scored his second goal of the night to put Ayr 2-1 up, we looked certain to take a lead to Edinburgh but the Hibs equaliser made the task look a little more daunting, with a trip to Easter Road still to negotiate. George Best did play in the first leg match but he was disinterested and did little to contribute to the match. The second leg saw the boys in black and white battle through with a stirring display that produced goals from Eric Morris and Derek Frye in extra-time to take us through to another semi-final.

Once more, we were one step away from our first national Final. Dundee FC stood in our way but I fancied our chances over the two legs of the semi-final. We had disposed of Hearts and Hibs, so there was no reason to fear Dundee. Ayr were once again disadvantaged by the draw and they would play the first leg at Somerset Park. It was important to take a lead to Dens Park but the match ended in a 1-1 draw. It was better than a defeat however and two weeks later there was everything to play for. We were one game away from a Cup Final…again.

My only consolation for not making it to Dundee for the second leg was the radio in my mum's kitchen. I had been bedridden for days with flu and there was no chance of me travelling anywhere. I sat at the kitchen table, with two of my brothers and my brother-in-law, listening to the commentary of the match on BBC Radio Scotland, praying for the right result. By the sound of things, Dundee were dominating the first half but although they had gone ahead, Gerry Christie equalised before half-time. Listening to the second half was nerve-racking stuff but Ayr did push forward more and when Billy McColl put Ayr ahead in the 58th minute, the radio went up in the air and was separated from the batteries when it crashed onto the floor. It took a full five minutes to reassemble the equipment and retune to the right station but all was well, we were ahead. It is amazing what a goal can do for medical ailments. My sore throat was feeling much better, my nasal congestion had disappeared and there was no headache for the first time in days. My mother popped her head around the door to comment, 'I thought you were ill'. My 'high' lasted until the 74th minute when Dundee made it 2-2 and despite the fact that Ayr created several chances in the last 15 minutes, it was Dundee who found a winner with five minutes to go. Denied the opportunity to support my team on the night and also denied the opportunity to buy my first-ever Cup Final ticket, my throat closed up again and my pounding headache returned. I went back to my bed, a man alone in illness and grief.

The pull of Ayr United was strong again but despite my new-found enthusiasm, time constraints and lack of funds would prevent my return to the fold. The beginning of 1981 saw big changes for me…again. My dad was selling his business and I was feeling the urge to be more independent. We had managed our two shops in Ayr's Westwood Crescent for four years before selling up in 1976 and buying an off licence, general grocer and newsagents business in Kilmarnock. Five years on and my dad was getting itchy feet again. He sold the shop in Craigie Road, Riccarton with a view to semi-retirement. He may have been 60 years old but the chances of him slowing down were remote.

No sooner had I secured a new job with Granada TV Rentals than old Joe had gone out and bought another similar shop in Kilmarnock, this time in Lainshaw Street. So he and my mum continued working together for the next six years, rising early in the morning for the newspaper deliveries and continuing with the seven days a week slog like they were a couple of young things. Meanwhile, in February 1981, after nine years in the family business, I had the luxury of a five-day-week from 8.45am till 5.30pm. No evening work, unlike the ridiculous hours I had found myself working in our shops. The only drawback in my job as a 'Multi-Purpose Representative' was Saturday working and no exceptions. That meant an end to amateur football and no full-time return to following Ayr United, at least in the short term. If I'm honest, I never felt entirely deprived. Perhaps it was maturity that was kicking in but in terms of priorities, earning a decent living and saving money was more important to me than following Ayr United all over Scotland and beyond.

At 26 years of age, I was eager to leave home and set up on my own, so I had to act more responsibly and pay more attention to my finances. Despite my relatively young age, I had experienced lots of life-changing situations and although football and Ayr United in particular had left an indelible mark on my life, there were many more non-sporting events to come that would shape me as a person. 1981 was a key year and joining Granada TV was a big move because it was then and there that I met Marilyn. My house hunting during the early months of 1982 saw me make a controversial move into my newly purchased flat in the dark shadow of Rugby Park... Kilmarnock. Number 1 Fairyhill Road was where I decided to mortgage myself up to the eyeballs and although I am extremely ashamed to admit that I made such a decision, it was purely financial. I simply could not afford to purchase a property in my home town at the time and so, I bit the bullet and moved up the road. If the truth be told, I only slept there. My nights out were always among my friends in Ayr and I was based in Ayr for my work.

The summer of 1982 was a big one for me. The excitement of a World Cup Finals was upon us and with the fiasco of Argentina four years old; I was looking forward to watching my two teams on the biggest stage of all. I was not particularly hopeful about Scotland's chances but I fancied Italy to see off the threat of holders Argentina, Germany and of course Brazil. As is customary on these occasions, Scotland botched it up with an embarrassing collision between Alan Hansen and Willie Miller resulting in a pantomime goal for the Soviet Union. Despite earning a 2-2 draw in that match, Scotland failed to qualify for the next round because of their inferior goal difference. The three points Scotland had earned in their group was the same total that Italy achieved, drawing three times, but the Italians scraped through to the next stage. That was a big relief for me because I had put my faith in my father's national team in the shape of a crisp £10 note at 20/1 on Italy to win the tournament. An unusual competition format saw Italy drawn in a group of three for round two. With Argentina and Brazil joining Italy, I had no doubt that my £10 had been a foolish investment. My brother Francis advised me to put another £10 on Italy as they looked good value at the updated odds of 40/1. He did not seem too keen on putting any money on himself and I certainly would not be wasting any more money on a disjointed, lethargic and de-motivated bunch of players.

I wish I had listened to him. Italy deservedly beat Argentina 2-1 before winning a classic match against Brazil, thanks to a Paulo Rossi hat-trick, in a 3-2 win. A straightforward 2-0 win against Poland in the semi-final took Italy into the Final to face a strong West Germany team. The entire Ferrara family gathered round the television at mum and dad's house for the big match and we celebrated wildly at the final whistle. A 3-1 win saw my dad pop the cork of the champagne bottle and I toasted my team's victory and my £200 windfall.

1983 was a momentous year for me. My personal life could not have been better. I was by then married to Marilyn and we had a beautiful baby boy. The fact that Ayr United had two horrendous seasons, narrowly avoiding relegation, finishing 12th in 1982-83 and again in 1983-84, was lost on me as I basked in the pleasure of my new son as he developed.

'Part-time supporter...you're just a part-time supporter...'

By 1985, the Ayr manager George Caldwell was not seeing any measure of success. Ayr had perhaps improved marginally but come May, they had finished only seventh in the First Division. After a poor start to the 1985-86 season the Ayr United board sacked him. The Caldwell reign was a miserable period but he did manage a 3-0 win against Kilmarnock before he went, so he was not all bad. To my delight, Ally MacLeod came back 'home' to take the helm and steady the ship...by May 1986, Ayr were relegated. The timing for an Ayr United depression could not have been more convenient for me. My daughter Madeleine was born in May 1985 and by the time the drop to Division Two came, I was too busy changing nappies and enjoying my growing family to get depressed about my team's nosedive into oblivion. It was by then seven years since Ayr united had graced the Premier League.

Despite the pleasure I was able to derive from my family life, the ignominy of relegation was hard to take.

1986-87 saw Ally MacLeod once more revive our fortunes to the point of a return to the relative respectability of the First Division. In fact, all that was required to achieve that target was a draw at home to Stirling Albion on the last day of the season. I invited my father-in-law, Gaetano Rossi (Tunny), to come to the match with me. This was a man who had experienced the glory years of his Celtic heroes, rubbing shoulders with the team and management of the European Champions era. Mr Rossi managed the Buchanan Restaurant in Buchanan Street in Glasgow and the Celtic players and officials frequented the establishment. He had plenty of anecdotes to call on from those days. He had some great stories about Bob Kelly, Jock Stein, the Lisbon Lions etc. He had been in Lisbon in 1967 to see Celtic lift the European Cup and now he was going to witness another landmark event, Ayr being promoted to the dizzy heights of the Scottish League First Division. My invitation was accepted and we took up our place on the north terracing at Somerset on the sunny afternoon that was 9 May 1987. Deep into the second half of that match depression had set in. We were down 3-0 in a match that required only one point for promotion. It was all over. When Ian McAllister pulled a goal back it meant nothing to me. Yes, Captain Courageous had started the comeback but it was not exactly Steven Gerrard in Istanbul in 2005. Nevertheless, 'Cally' had not given up, even if I had. The second from John Sludden offered a slight glimmer of hope though and the whole crowd warmed to the fight-back that was now underway. I then experienced one of the most excruciating moments of my time following Ayr United. United were piling on the pressure in the few remaining minutes of the match, as Stirling Albion tried to hold on for a victory that could mean promotion for them. Ayr's left-back, Craig Buchanan, received a pass just level with our position on the terracing. He moved forward with the ball and from 30 yards out he let go a thunderbolt shot. I heard myself scream 'yesssss' as the ball headed for the top corner of the net. The goalkeeper never got near it but the rising shot smacked off the top of the bar and continued its journey high into the crowd behind the goal. A couple of inches lower and we were going up but sadly it was not to be. My father-in-law turned towards me with his head in his hands, 'Oh no, I don't believe it,' he said. He had been engulfed by the occasion and carried along on the tide of emotion that was evident inside Somerset Park. There were no more chances and the look on his face when the final whistle went, told me that he was almost as gutted as I was. As the disconsolate Ayr support filed out in silence, after applauding the efforts of the Ayr fight-back, the Stirling Albion fans 'invaded' the park and were dancing and singing inside the penalty area at the Railway end of the ground. It was short-lived though. The celebration came to an abrupt halt when the news filtered through that Raith Rovers had won 4-1 against Stranraer to win promotion on goal difference. Ayr and Stirling had both lost out on the last day of the season. There was a certain degree of satisfaction to be derived from the reaction of my father-in-law to the events in the closing stages and his obvious disappointment that Ayr had lost the match and failed in their bid for promotion. He had good reason to support Celtic. As an Arsenal supporting Londoner who had moved to Glasgow in 1950 with his new wife, a born and bred Glaswegian, he had been influenced by his in-laws' allegiance to the green side of the Old Firm and his first-hand experience of hosting the Celtic squad in his restaurant had served to consolidate that affiliation. Nevertheless, here he was aligning himself with the Ayr United cause and although my attempts to indoctrinate him would have been futile, I would like to think that he had a wee soft spot for our team from that day on.

The patience of the Ayr support was rewarded the following season when the team made it back into the First Division with a season apparently filled with top-notch entertainment and superb attacking football. I say apparently because I missed almost all of it. Marilyn and I opened our business in June 1987 so while Henry Templeton ran defences ragged and John Sludden rattled in the goals, I managed only a handful of matches as we established our restaurant and shop business. The news of David Murray's potential takeover of the club seemed to capture the imagination of everyone associated with Ayr United but it eventually came to nothing. The perception among the Ayr support seemed to be that this was a great opportunity but to be frank, none of us knew what was going on behind the scenes. When the going got tough in the talks between the two parties, Murray did make a statement saying that he, '…would not be going away,' suggesting that he was going to do whatever it took to gain control of the club. He portrayed himself as a lifelong supporter of the club and then promptly jumped ship to form an allegiance with his new love, Glasgow Rangers. His treachery was laid bare for everyone to see and I for one will not forgive him.

Having accepted redundancy packages from our jobs with Granada TV,

Marilyn and I set up the Four Seasons restaurant and shop business on Ayr seafront. I could say that we were influenced by the famous New York restaurant of the same name but we decided it would be an apt name for the business because on Ayr beach we could expect spring, summer, autumn and winter all in one day. Saturday afternoon radio was my only lifeline to Ayr United unless I happened to bump into someone who had been at the game. It was like a trip back to 1971 and the BBC Teleprinter, only without the picture.

In the years between 1981 and 1987, I had continued to play pub football on a Sunday but by the end of that period I had reached the grand old age of 32 and although decent players would maybe get away with playing for an extra couple of seasons, I was a bad enough player without factoring in my physical deterioration. My playing career ended in 1987. I called it a day after two seasons playing and managing an Italian team called SFIDA, which played in a league with teams from all over the West of Scotland. This was probably the most laid-back football experience of a playing career at the very...bottom.

A Cup Final For Ally

And a Management Merry-Go-Round

As our new business settled down and we became accustomed to our busy lives, my thoughts turned once again to Ayr United and the serious business of supporter recruitment. With my playing career well and truly over, the last refuge I had in the world, in a football context, was going to be watching Ayr United and as a married man with a growing family, I felt compelled to turn my attention to indoctrinating my family in the ways of the 'Honest Men'. My son Nicholas's first match was at Somerset Park in April 1989, just before his sixth birthday. I took him along with me to a Dunfermline match. Ayr lost 2-1 but it was quite a good game and I spent most of the afternoon explaining everything that was going on to my wee fellow who was not at all interested in the football. He did ask one question, 'Daddy, why are the people in the Wendy House singing songs?' 'The 'Wendy House' was the title he had decided to give the covered enclosure at the Somerset Road end of the ground. He never did take to football in any serious way and perhaps wisely, he gave himself less grief by pursuing his passion for music in the years ahead. I'm absolutely sure that he is glad about the choices he made. For me, it was one battle lost and strangely enough two to go.

Nicholas chose to go to his cousin Kieron's birthday party on Sunday 11 November 1990 instead of coming with his mum, dad and sister to the B&Q Centenary Cup Final that day. Marilyn, five-year-old Madeleine and I travelled to Fir Park, Motherwell for another one of those great days out. We had the flags, there was the singing, the banter with the Dundee fans and Ally MacLeod had once again taken us as close to our wee bit of glory as we could have hoped for. Unfortunately, we had the Cup torn from our grasp by Billy Dodds, who scored a hat-trick on the day, as Ayr lost 3-2 after extra-time. I can still picture from that day, the bizarre sight of the guy on stilts dressed as a mum, pushing a giant pram with another man inside the pram, dressed as a baby. Everything about the day was great, apart from the result.

The match itself entertained an 11,500 crowd and the Ayr supporters were buoyant in a one-sided first half. When Ian McAllister, the Ayr captain, slammed the ball home after a 12th minute corner had dropped to him, I imagined the same player lifting the cup above his head at the end of the match. Ayr dominated the first half and there was every reason to believe that we would go all the way. The pattern in the second half was completely different and every time Colin West or Billy Dodds got the ball for Dundee, I went into panic mode. It was a few minutes into the second half when Jim McCann, our solid left-back, was guilty of a rash challenge, barging West inside the box. There could be no complaints about the penalty award and Dodds sent David Purdie the wrong way from the penalty spot to equalise. Twenty minutes later and I was sitting with my head in my hands when Dodds headed home a cross from West to put Dundee in front. I was probably one of many who had that sick feeling in the pit of my stomach knowing that the match was running away from us but when big David Smyth's shot deflected off a Dundee defender and looped over the 'keeper and into the net, I dared to believe again. Thirty minutes of nerve tingling extra-time and with 10 minutes left of the second period, my daughter Madeleine could wait no longer. 'I need to take her to the toilet,' said Marilyn. They were still gone when, with five minutes left, Dodds won the cup for Dundee when he slid the ball home from the edge of the box. That sickly feeling returned again and when the final whistle blew, I made my way to the exit only to meet the two other members of my family on the way back in, oblivious to the catastrophe that had unfolded in their absence.

On reflection, it had been a great match, Ayr had gone down battling and overall, despite the bitter disappointment of defeat, it was an occasion to remember. The disappointment of our Cup Final defeat was compounded a few weeks later when we witnessed the end of an era. The man who was probably the most influential figure in Ayr United's history, Ally MacLeod, decided to call it a day on my birthday, 8 December after making an absolutely tremendous contribution during his three stints managing Ayr United between 1966 and 1990. How would the club follow the class act that was Ally? The job was handed to George Burley. His first opportunity in management was to be back in his native Ayrshire and I for one was delighted with the appointment, particularly since he would continue in a playing capacity. There was no doubting his quality as a footballer. It is my strong belief that to be a successful manager of a team like Ayr United, we do not exactly have the cream of the crop in our playing squad, the most important quality required is an ability to motivate people. I was not privy to George's team talks or his one to one interaction with players but he certainly never came across as a man-manager, a motivator of people. It is perhaps an unfair comparison, and I am not sure how Ally MacLeod went about his job, but he could definitely make the most ordinary player produce the most extraordinary performance. On the plus side, I always admired George as a player and I thought that he did a reasonable job as Ayr manager. The results may not have been wonderful but I felt that he was taking us in the right direction. OK, he was not Ally MacLeod but if we had known who was to follow him we would have been down on our knees, begging George Burley's forgiveness for sacking him.

Burley had been in the Ayr United job for almost a year when the final piece of the Ferrara family jigsaw was put in place. Ben arrived on 6 December 1991 to complete our family of three children. With two boys and one girl, I felt entitled to believe that I could turn one of my boys into an Ayr fan and having failed miserably with Nicky, Ben was my great hope. However, it was early days in terms of his indoctrination. We also had another mouth to feed and a seven-days-a-week business to run. There was plenty to think about other than the depressing circumstances surrounding

Ayr United. In terms of results, finishing in 12th, sixth and seventh place in the First Division, in the three seasons George Burley was involved, was not exactly something to get excited about but to be fair, the club was not exactly awash with cash to bring in new players. Nevertheless, more was expected and the club's directors believed that it was someone other than Burley who was required. By Christmas 1993 he was gone. He may not have been Mr Personality but I thought he should have been given more time.

It was ironic that we had named our business 'The Four Seasons' because it was the seasonal influences on the business that made up our minds to sell up and move on. We may have joked about rain, sun and snow all in one day but the business was reliant on temperate weather to ensure success. From April to September we made good money, working 15-hour days, only to see our resources diminish during the winter months. We put the business up for sale and only a few days later, an Indian businessman walked unannounced into the restaurant to open negotiations. Two subsequent visits later and we instructed our lawyer to make the deal. Marilyn returned to her long-term career in retail management when Granada TV asked her to return and I rented two units, to sell toys, in what was marketed as a new quality shopping experience in Ayr's Arran Mall. It turned out to be a dowdy indoor marketplace and after only a few months it was obvious that it would not last. What now? By August 1994 I had enrolled in a business course at college with a view to a completely new career in paid employment. My undistinguished academic past had caught up with me and, after the prodding and pushing of my wife and mother-in-law, I went back to school. It is still hard to believe that my wife worked full time and looked after our three children while supporting me through college and university. Between getting my head down to study and working nightshift at weekends and weekday evenings at the Tesco store in Whitletts Road in Ayr, I contributed very little to family life. It was study, fill shelves, sleep. I hated that job but it was not all doom and gloom. We knew why we were doing it. We figured that a few years of hard work and gritted teeth, with the promise of stability for our family, would be worth it.

Attending the Ayr United home football matches was my escape from the pressures of studying and Tesco but in truth that only increased the stress. This torture was psychological. The new Ayr United manager certainly had personality. He could also be described as stylish, likeable, confident and a good communicator. What a mistake it was to employ him. Player-manager, Simon Stainrod was a decent player but past his best, he was a showman and most importantly he was a millinery expert. The fedora wearing stunts were terribly amusing but I do not particularly want to take up space with any more details of his time in charge. Suffice to say, the team survived in the First Division in the season he took over and we were relegated to the Second Division in his first full season. Fortunately, Bill Barr, the club chairman, dispatched Stainrod early in the 1995-96 Second Division campaign. Ayr 1 Berwick 4, followed by Ayr 1 Forfar 3, said it all really...next!

A New Era and a New Recruit

By 1996, my playing career was a distant memory but a story relayed to me by my nephew, Anthony, brought back memories of some great fun I had at Dam Park Hall. Nowadays, there is no building in the area where the hall stood. Next to the river, there is now only a car park that serves Ayr College. It may have been the place where I had my teeth knocked halfway down my throat in 1977 but it was also a fun-filled palace of football every Christmas and Easter. Nineteen years after my opponent punched my teeth in, Anthony was still able to enjoy his five-a-side tournament football just as I did. Nothing had changed in all that time. It was still a large damp, freezing cold hangar and the games were played on a concrete surface. There was none of your third generation astro-grass here. Tony, as he is known by his cohort of friends, dreamt up a practical joke that brought chaos to the tournament and left every player in the hall totally confused and bewildered by his tomfoolery. He was very familiar with the tournament set-up and he decided it would be a wheeze to take advantage of the organisers by registering two teams under the names 'Pitch A' and

'Pitch B'. He and his friends then carried out their usual routine, changing into their strips at the side of the hall and discussing tactics for the upcoming group matches. The other boys in the team were perplexed as to why he would attach these ridiculous names to the teams but they let him carry on, knowing that he had hatched a plan that would most probably have a hysterical conclusion. Once Johnny Hubbard had carried out the final preparations, the public address system burst into life to announce the first round of matches to take place on the three pitches that sat side by side along the length of the hall. 'OK everyone, the draw has been made and the first games will be as follows…on pitch A, Mossblown versus Pitch B… on Pitch B, Pitch A versus Troon Thistle and on pitch C, Mainholm Thistle versus Carrick United.' After a great deal of repetition from the announcer and some serious head scratching, the teams finally managed to kick-off but there was even more fun after another few rounds of matches. The announcer was oblivious to the confusion as he was simply calling out the fixtures by reading from the sheet in front of him. It went like this… 'On Pitch A, Belmont versus Troon Thistle…On Pitch B, Pitch A versus Pitch B…on Pitch C, blah, blah, blah.' By the time he had reached the fixtures for pitch C, nobody had a clue what was going on. Meanwhile, Tony and his mates were bent double laughing instead of taking up their positions on the pitch. I do not expect Johnny Hubbard or the announcer saw the funny side of that incident but there should always be a place for some fun alongside the football.

A new era was dawning for Ayr United. Exciting times were just around the corner and it quickly became apparent that Gordon Dalziel was the man for the job. In his first full season in charge he took the team to the 1996-97 Second Division title. As an Ayr supporter spoiled by past seasons competing at the top level of Scottish football, I never saw the Second Division title as any great achievement. I was one of a large number of Ayr fans who were of the opinion that we should never have been down there in the first place. My highlights of that 1996-97 season were our away trips to Kilmarnock and Rangers in the Coca Cola sponsored League Cup. The second round tie against Killie had been fairly even until Bobby Connor scored a cracker to silence the Rugby Park faithful and take Ayr through to meet Rangers in the third round. A 20-year-old Mark Roberts played for Killie that night and the wee so-and-so dived in vain to claim a penalty. He would later become an 'Honest Man' and all would be forgiven but after that night he was roundly abused by Ayr supporters during his stints at Airdrie, Partick Thistle and St Mirren for the crime of simulation and the more serious offence of apparently being a 'Dirty Killie *******'. It was a hard fought win with Stevie Kerrigan running the Kilmarnock defence ragged and wee Isaac English controlling the midfield with Connor, as an irate, red-faced Alex Totten raged on the touchline.

The third round draw gave us a trip to Ibrox and a trip to the home of either of the two 'ugly sisters' of Scottish football was to be relished. Having begged a lift from Ronnie and Charlie Johnston in a van, seven of us made our way up to Glasgow with great expectations. On paper we had absolutely no chance but the game was to be on grass so we felt that we could pull off a surprise victory. We arrived in the south side of the city in plenty of time and, on the advice of someone in the group, our driver parked the van in a street that sat on the other side of the motorway from Ibrox stadium. No sooner had we stopped than the resident of the large house we were parked outside came out for a word. 'I see by your scarves you're Ayr supporters boys...' he said before continuing, '...here's a wee bit of advice fellas, don't park there because as soon as the game starts, the tow trucks will be out in force and they'll lift any vehicle they find on this road'. As we considered our next move, the householder added, 'Stick your van on my driveway, it'll be safe there and out of the way'. He turned out to be a real decent guy who saved us a lot of money. As we made our way towards Ibrox, across the footbridge over the motorway, there were people parking cars all the way down the road. We did say to several of them that they could have their cars towed but nobody paid any attention.

Apparently, the mountain Ayr United had to climb that night was not quite steep enough, so fate took a hand. We arrived in the stadium in a fairly buoyant mood only to feel bewildered by the team announcements. Two of Ayr's heroes in the last round at Rugby Park were not mentioned, not even on the bench. Stevie Kerrigan and Isaac English both fell ill ahead of the match and were withdrawn from the squad. The idea that we could win the match was fanciful before this news and the task had now turned to 'Mission Impossible'. Ayr defended gallantly in the first half and managed to go in at the break level at 0-0. The second half began with Rangers laying siege to the Ayr goal and the big-money stars finally got their act together to take the lead in 48 minutes. Paul Gascoigne set the ball up for Jorge Albertz to hammer home an unstoppable shot from 25 yards. The Ayr crowd would not admit defeat and the players responded to the marvellous backing they got by hitting back. Twelve minutes later, Paul Kinnaird slung a tempting cross into the Rangers box and Darren Henderson bundled the ball home. Unbelievably, at 1-1, Ayr had a chance to go in front when Willie Jamieson headed past the post but when Rangers won a free kick on the edge of the Ayr box with 10 minutes to go we were all justifiably worried. Henry Smith, the Ayr goalkeeper, was still lining up his defensive 'wall' when 'Gazza' took a quick free kick to put Rangers 2-1 up. The Ayr support tried to rally the team for the final few minutes but Derek McInnes finished it off with a goal in the last minute to make the final score Rangers 3 Ayr United 1. Our boys had put up a great fight, despite losing two of our players before the game had even started. I suppose it is a good sign when you are disappointed to lose to a team costing millions of pounds but that is the lot of provincial club football fans. It is important to be philosophical in these situations.

When we returned to the van after the match, we found the street full of people who could not understand where their cars had gone. Just as we had been told, the tow trucks had been busy during the 90 minutes of the match and it was going to be an expensive night out for some of the travelling Ayr support. Sure enough, a story in the *Ayrshire Post* on the week following the match described in detail how the money making exercise had rolled into action to catch out the unsuspecting fans. One of the Ayr supporters suckered was John McGinn. The *Ayrshire Post* story the following week described how John had to shell out £105 to get his car back and a further £20 for his parking fine. His total outlay to follow his team for one match was £158. He had contributed to what amounted to a nice little earner for the local authority, at the expense of decent folk looking for a night's entertainment.

For me, it was all happening on every front. Ayr were back in the First Division, I had completed my HND in Business Administration, Ben, my younger son, was already fanatical about football at the tender age of five, and to my surprise Madeleine, my 11-year-old daughter was also taking a real interest in football. During my two years at Ayr College, one of my lecturers, Shelagh McLachlan, introduced me to a guidance software package called 'Adult Directions'. It consisted of answering around 100 questions about aspects of work and it produced a list of suitable careers based on the answers given. Careers Officer was number six on the list and when I read the details of what was involved in the job, I decided to pursue it. I was preparing my application to articulate to the final year of the University of Paisley Business Management Degree at the Ayr campus but on the advice of David Clark, the manager at Ayr Careers office, and after spending some time 'shadowing' Careers Officers doing the job, I instead applied for the Postgraduate Diploma in Careers Guidance at the Paisley campus of the university. I never thought that I would be accepted without first obtaining my degree but David had advised me that if they thought I had the ability, they would accept me. It was important to get back into the world of work as soon as possible, so the opportunity to avoid another year of study was one I had to take. I got my place on the course and started in September 1996. By the end of Ayr's successful Second Division campaign, I had graduated with my Postgraduate Diploma in Careers Guidance and I was on the lookout for an opportunity to embark on a new career and an escape from the purgatory that was Tesco.

Meanwhile, another member of my family was developing as a football star and was in fact soon to become an Ayr United player. I never fulfilled my dream of pulling on the black and white of Ayr United as a player but I was very proud when one of my children gained that distinction. While I felt fairly confident about turning Ben into an Ayr supporter, it had never occurred to me that Madeleine could be my big recruitment success story. Not only did she fall in love with Ayr United but she also played for them. It may have been Ayr United Girls under-13 team but it was Ayr United nevertheless and I was suitably proud of her. She spent two years playing with the club and at the end of her first season she was awarded the Player of the Year trophy at the annual presentation. After a short career with Ayr United she concentrated more on her netball. She had developed her netball skills at St John's Primary and went on to represent Queen Margaret Academy and Ayrshire Schools in the years ahead. She had her sights set on playing for Scotland, an achievement of her mum's some years previously, but it was not to be.

Madeleine's love of football was not diminished after leaving Ayr United Girls and she started coming to Ayr United matches with me. I never pushed hard to get her on board. In fact, Madeleine asked to come to a match with me and I was certain she would soon become bored and refuse to return. It was probably my sexist attitude that led me to believe that and in hindsight, I got it completely wrong. From the age of 12 until she left for university five years later, she accompanied me to most games, home and away and, much to my surprise, she loved it. Her timing was perfect. She was royally entertained as Ayr enjoyed a good measure of success, in relative terms, between 1997 and 2002. Along with our young friends Simon Ward and David Bonsor, we travelled up and down the country following our team. Although my obsession with being involved in a practical sense finally saw me return to play an active part in football as a coach in 1997, I still managed to fit it in with following Ayr United, as the games rarely clashed.

1997-98 was to be a satisfactory season for Ayr United and this coincided with achieving the stability we craved in our family's personal life. Dalziel consolidated Ayr's presence in the First Division with a decent seventh place finish and I had a short spell at British Aerospace as a Project Co-ordinator for the Jetstream Cessation Programme. I was part of a team that was employed to deal with the transition of 380 workers facing redundancy. Although it was a very stressful time for those people losing their jobs, around 85% were assisted in finding alternative employment, so it was not all doom and gloom. The temporary nature of my work meant that I was still on the lookout for my first job as a Careers Adviser but I was not exactly spoilt for choice. When the support programme at British Aerospace ended, I successfully applied for the Project Manager position at the Signposts Project, an employment initiative, in Maybole and took up my position in June 1998. It was a local project overseen by a committee consisting of local councillors, businessmen and community activists. I had only been in the job for six months when the decision was taken to 'mainline' the project and I therefore became a South Ayrshire Council employee. It increased my salary substantially and I enjoyed the job so much that I stayed there for 10 years, helping people with job search, CV preparation, interview skills, careers advice, motivation and confidence building. I also held classes at Carrick Academy to assist with the transition of fourth, fifth and sixth year students from school to employment, training or education. A big bonus was that the office was open Monday to Friday, so my weekends were free to pursue my obsession with football.

Back to My Youth

My introduction to youth football coaching and management was, I suspect, similar to that of many others who have taken on a similar role. Ben had been kicking a ball since learning how to walk and by the age of five he was more than ready to join an organised set up where he could learn more than I was able to teach him. Although I had coaching and management experience from my amateur days, I had never seen myself as having any particular expertise in that side of the game. I was always just an enthusiastic supporter and a player prepared to work hard at my favourite pastime, which has admittedly become a lifelong obsession. My only intention at that time was to see Ben interacting with other kids and developing his skills. He was painfully shy and said very little outside of the family circle and this seemed like the perfect opportunity to get him out of his shell. Football was the carrot and although I believed that he may be reluctant to join a club, I need not have worried. He was desperate to get started. I made a few phone calls and discovered that a club called Valspar held coaching sessions for youngsters at Mainholm Academy on Friday evenings. New trainers, football boots, socks, shorts, Ayr United replica top (gimme a break, it was my one indulgence) and we were ready to go.

Note: In a show of commitment to Ayr United supporter recruitment and in the spirit of treating my children equally, I felt obliged to buy Ben an Ayr United strips. I had previously attempted the replica strips stunt with Nicky when he was younger. He let out a scream of apparent joy on opening one of his Christmas presents before proclaiming the arrival of '…an Ayr United strips…yessssss!' On reflection, he was probably just humouring me.

I pulled up in the school car park on a Friday evening in January 1997 still harbouring concerns about whether or not Ben would get out of the car. As soon as I pulled the handbrake on, the back door of the car opened and off he went following on behind the other kids walking towards the entrance to the school at the side of the building. As a protective parent, I worried about who I was leaving him with but my apprehension disappeared when I saw my old teammate walking over to greet us. Colin Dodds, my Kyle Thistle colleague from the 70s was coaching the kids alongside his brother Lee and I had no reservations about leaving Ben in his care. I completed Ben's registration and then headed off, returning an hour later to find Ben, red faced and his hair matted with sweat. It had been quite a session for him and he slept well that night. Ben's Friday nights became the highlight of his week and the fact that he was a year younger than the others did not seem to bother him.

He had been at the club for six weeks when, one Friday evening, I arrived to pick him up after a session. A heavyset man in his 30s approached me as I stood watching the final five-a-side match of the evening from the gym entrance. He introduced himself as the manager of the team that Ben was apparently now part of. 'The wee fella' needs to be at Shoot Super Soccer for half past nine tomorrow morning'. I explained that Ben was only at the club to train and was not ready to play in games yet. 'Och don't worry, he'll be fine,' the large chap said. Needless to say, Ben was ecstatic. After a bath and several attempts to get him to bed, I finally discovered a strategy to control my youngest. I had a new threat that I could hang over him. 'Do as I say or there will be no football tomorrow.' That threat worked really well as a child management tool over the years. On this Friday night it was all about him getting some sleep and my blackmail was very effective. Marilyn found the whole situation partly hilarious and partly worrying. It was her precious wee boy pulling on a football strips and actually playing for a team, at the tender age of five years and nine months. 'Do you think he'll be alright?' she asked me. I just repeated what the Valspar coach had said to me...'Och don't worry, he'll be fine'.

Ben had his kit bag packed and was ready to leave the house for 8 o'clock the next morning. Considering that it would take me 10 minutes to drive to the Whitletts complex and we were to be there for 9.30, it was safe to assume that Ben was up for it. 'I stayed awake all night,' he declared. A slight exaggeration but nevertheless it did illustrate his excitement about participating in his first big sporting event. His football obsession was now well established and it's a fascination that has stayed with him all these years. I had one reservation about the whole Valspar set up and that was the way the coach spoke to the kids. From my perspective on the outside of the caged playing area, I could clearly hear what he was shouting at the players and every second word was a swear word. At half-time, should the team be behind, the kids got a rollicking and his diatribe was always spattered with Fs, Bs and Cs. A bit much for a five-year-old to handle but Ben had turned six by then so everything would be fine. I do not think he was such a bad bloke, it was just the way he communicated with everyone. Some of the opposing coaches made complaints to the league organiser, Johnny Hubbard, after witnessing the coach's outrageous outbursts but several warnings later and no positive change had occurred in the coach's behaviour. Something had to give and one Saturday morning Davy Agnew appeared beside me at the perimeter wall as Ben's game was in full flow.

Note: Yes, the same Davy Agnew who punched my lights out at Dam Park hall in 1977.

He asked me if I was aware of the complaints that had been made about the abusive style of the team coach. I had no sooner acknowledged this when he fired in a direct request, 'How about taking over the team?' he asked. I never needed to think about it, 'I did my bit with the amateurs Davy and this is not something I could take on'. He seemed to accept my decision, 'No problem, it looks like the team will need to fold though, he's not being allowed to take the team anymore. I don't suppose you could do me a favour could you?' He followed up his question immediately with another 'Could you take the team for a couple of weeks so that I can at least try to find someone else to take the kids?' Call me naïve or gullible but I agreed. After all, a couple of weeks? It's not exactly a big commitment. Eleven years later I was becoming disillusioned with youth football management and I made the decision to pack it in.

So, six days after my short conversation with Davy, the advice I was given went something like this, 'Remember to contact the council to change the school "let" into your name. Don't let the players take their strips after games, they'll forget to bring them back...and don't forget the Valspar meetings are the second Tuesday of every month'. Why would I change the billing name and address to mine if I was only holding the fort for a couple of weeks? I had to attend the club meetings every month even though I was only doing this job for a fortnight. I suppose that, subconsciously, I knew what I was taking on and it was never going to be a short term, temporary role. After undertaking the SFA Early Touches coaching course I was raring to go and the idea of taking 'my' kids through the age groups, competing with teams from all over Ayrshire, watching them develop skills and experience as well as friendship and community spirit really appealed to me. Initially, I was on my own as a coach and the number of kids registered with the club grew quickly. The problem was that every time a mother or father turned up on a training night with their wee boy or girl, I never had the heart to turn them away. Young Simon Ward had been bringing along his younger brother to the club and he began helping out with some of the training exercises. He had taken his first coaching qualifications and he proved to be a good help to me. As the weeks progressed, he started taking half of the group while I took the other half and by the summer we had decided to register two teams for the following season, so that all the kids could enjoy playing matches. We set up matches between the two groups and although Simon's team struggled initially, they would benefit from a season in the league in much the same way as my group of players did in the season just finished.

Our team developed really well during their first competitive season and they won the vast majority of matches. I say competitive but the league was actually non-competitive. The scores were not recorded and the league competition was trophy free. I had learned a lot in the previous season and I intended to give due consideration to all the players I came into contact with. I found all the managers in the older age group courteous, friendly and sympathetic to my cause, in relation to developing the skills of my players. Many of them took the time to encourage our players and some even tried to ensure that our kids got a goal to celebrate. On one occasion, we travelled to Troon to play the local club and after losing our fourth goal, their manager took off two outfield players and later their goalkeeper so that the game was more of a match. If only every youth football manager had that attitude, we could then contribute to the development of all the kids in our care. In our second season, I took account of the youngsters in the other team and tried to replicate the consideration shown to our team the previous season. Regrettably, a high number of the managers and coaches I came to know in my second season with the club had an altogether different, more ruthless approach. The monthly West of Scotland league meetings, held at the Ex-Servicemen's Club in Ayr's Alloway Place, brought together team managers and there was always chat and banter before and after proceedings. I remember one encounter with a fellow manager that typified the attitude of many others I had the misfortune of knowing. I had opened up our conversation with, 'Hi there, how are you? How's your team getting on?' The reply said it all. 'We've played 16 games, won 15, drawn 1 and lost none, we've scored 83 goals and conceded 11.' I wanted to ask him for a little more detail but I think the sarcasm would have been lost on him. He never asked me about my team as it was of no interest to him. I do not believe that this type of person is particularly interested in his own players, never mind the opposition team. It was all about him. There are people in positions of authority and influence in youth football who abuse that status for their own ends. It is disappointing that they are attracted to the game because they do little to enhance the development of youth football in this country. It is not all bad however. In my youth football management days I also met some considerate, decent, well-meaning people that I had a lot of time for. In fact, there are a number of people I consider friends to this day.

One person, whom it was my good fortune to meet, was Billy Walker. He was the manager-coach of Cumnock Juniors Boys Club 1991 team. The year group indicated the year of birth for players registered and Billy's son was born in the same year as Ben, hence the reason we both found ourselves coaching at that level. Billy's philosophy for running his team was very similar to my own. We worked with the players we had and adopted a community club approach to our voluntary positions. I never saw the attraction in seeking out better players to replace the kids I had at the club. Instead, I focused on improving the players I had and I know Billy had the same attitude. Other managers in the same age group had a more ruthless approach. As our teams progressed through the age groups we would commiserate with one another when a player was 'tapped up' and subsequently left to join another team. Another view I shared with the Cumnock coach was that, although I wanted my team to win, it was not everything. I remember Valspar beating Cumnock Juniors 7-2 in one match and after the game Billy and I had a chat about what went right and wrong for our respective teams before wishing one another luck for our upcoming games. Cumnock Juniors had their fair share of victories over our team also but I found it easy to be magnanimous in these situations. If the mutual respect that existed between us could have been replicated throughout our league it would have been beneficial for all concerned but unfortunately, losing was not acceptable to some of the managers at our level.

On balance, I was having a ball. Earning a decent living in a job I loved, happy to be involved in youth football, watching our family develop and supporting a revitalised Ayr United with Madeleine, my new football buddy. Life was fun.

Cup Fever

In the next few seasons, Madeleine and the other youngsters joined me in experiencing some of the most enjoyable cup ties we could have hoped for, starting with a battle against Kilmarnock in the fourth round of the Scottish Cup in 1998. Torrential rain had fallen on Ayr in the run up to the match in mid-February and it continued during the game. The soft-going, coupled with the fiercely contested nature of the match, resulted in the pitch turning into a mud heap. The Ayr support could not have asked for a more committed and passionate display from the 'Honest Men' against a Kilmarnock team that would go on to secure a fourth place finish in the SPL and qualification for the UEFA Cup. A 2-0 victory was Ayr's, thanks to a battling team display and goals from Jim Dick and Ian Ferguson. The Somerset Road end of the ground was in raptures when Laurent Djaffo stole the ball from Jim Lachlan and passed to Ferguson who turned before slotting the ball past Gordon Marshall. The packed terracing behind the goal was the place to be. I was jumping up and down like a young thing, hugging Madeleine and anyone else who was up for a cuddle. I was back to my youth, joining in with the chant of 'Easy, easy, easy...' OK, so we were hammered 4-1 by Hearts in the next round, but it took nothing away from the derby win.

The team's win at Motherwell in August of the same year saw Ayr United developing a taste for cup football again. On a Tuesday night at Fir Park, Glynn Hurst was on fire. He almost burst the net with the opening goal and followed that by outpacing the Motherwell defence before sliding the ball across goal for Shaun Teale to beat his own 'keeper to give Ayr a 2-0 win in the fourth round of the League Cup. Rangers had a little too much for us in the quarter-final, beating us 2-0 at Somerset Park, but we were definitely a cup team not to be taken lightly.

When the Scottish Cup draw was made for the third round of the 1998-99 season's tournament, the whole of Ayr was relishing yet another chance to put one over on our county rivals. Ahead of matches like these there is understandably a certain air of apprehension. I mean, let's be sensible, we were a mid-table First Division team playing a team who were flying in the division above. A repeat of the previous season's heroics may have been unlikely but ahead of the game against Killie I was as bullish as any other inhabitant of the Auld Toon. The condition of Somerset Park on 23 January 1999 was a whole lot better this time around. If Kilmarnock slipped up this time, there could be no excuses. The playing surface was perfect. My Killie-supporting acquaintances were predicting a slaughter and as the whistle sounded for the start of the match, any confidence I had earlier, disappeared completely. I did not fancy us at all. However, as the lyrics of a George Michael song go '...I gotta have faith...' How could I ever have doubted the lads? It may have been a fortuitous break of the ball that set up Andy Lyons for the opener but he fairly hammered in his shot from the edge of the penalty area after half an hour. Cue bedlam in the Somerset Road end, the north terrace and the main stand and enclosure as, at the opposite end of the ground, the Killie fans indulged in a game of 'Statues' I used to enjoy playing that game as a child. The music would stop and, at that very moment, to prevent being knocked out of the game, I would do my very best to stand motionless. From my usual position to the left of the goal at the Somerset Road end, I observed that the Kilmarnock support was expert at the parlour game. The question was, could we hold onto the lead for another 60 minutes? I need not have worried. Not only was our defence solid, but Glynn Hurst and company had the Kilmarnock rearguard chasing shadows. Ray Montgomerie may have had a big height advantage over 'Hursty' but the big man panicked every time the ball was played to Ayr's front line. It was a long ball forward that led to Ayr's second goal. When the two players challenged for a high ball, late in the second half, Hurst probably impeded Montgomerie by putting his arm across the Killie player's face and perhaps the Ayr player was also guilty of pulling his opponents shirt. It's also true that maybe the Killie number four did not actually cause the Ayr striker to go to ground...but to my mind it was definitely a penalty and a sending off. Andy Walker blasted the ball home from the spot and we were all belting out 'Ayr, Ayr, Super Ayr'. Two goals to the good, 80 minutes gone and there was now no possibility that Kilmarnock would get back into the game. It could not get any better than this. Well, that's not strictly true. It could and it did. With seven minutes remaining, Gary Teale was next to make his mark. He outpaced the Kilmarnock defence and when he went down in the box there could be no doubt that, this time, it was a genuine penalty. Gordon Marshall had the unenviable task of facing Andy Walker for the second time. The Ayr player was already in party mood and it was time for a little showboating. The Killie 'keeper guessed the ball would go to his right and when Walker chipped the ball straight down the middle, Marshall was too late to make a correction. All he could do was claw the air and watch as the ball bobbed into the empty net where he stood a second earlier. Andy Walker, in the twilight of his career, had brought so much to Ayr United as a player and everyone associated with the club would always remember him fondly. His outrageous penalty kick elevated him to the status of legend in the eyes of the Ayr United faithful. As the chants of 'Easy, easy, easy' subsided, we all floated out of Somerset Park after the final whistle, having given the team a standing ovation. It is the kind of celebration that comes easy to home supporters as we are already standing. The songs and chants from the away support of 'Paper Noses' and 'Somerset's a piggery' had been replaced by...silence. On this particular occasion, the Killie supporters had also indulged in their whimsical comedy routine of wearing facemasks to make their point but I saw no evidence of them as we left the ground.

The harsh fact is that no matter how rundown Ayr's home ground is, Rugby Park could never create an atmosphere to match Somerset Park. The sterile, haunted, plastic structures that constitute modern football stadia have sucked the atmosphere out of Scottish football. I for one hope that Ayr United continue to play at Tryfield Place and I would advocate a refurbishment of the stadium as opposed to a move to Heathfield, or anywhere else. That cup campaign ended in quarter-final disappointment at Tannadice, when we lost 2-1 to Dundee United in a replay, after holding them to a 0-0 draw at Somerset. Nevertheless, it was a great effort from the team to get to that stage.

Things got even more dramatic for us in 2000 with yet another great Scottish Cup run for the 'Honest Men' and our small group were there for every kick of the ball, home and away. We travelled up to Dundee on 29 January for the third round match and the team did enough, with a 0-0 draw, to bring Dundee back to Somerset Park for a replay. Because of the weather, the replay never took place until 15 February but what a night we had. The now eight-year-old Ben came along with us to that one. That gave me the opportunity to bring him into the Ayr United fold. We were huddled together under the Somerset Road end enclosure, wrapped up in our coats, scarves and gloves and we were still freezing with the cold. The pitch was covered with snow but the game went ahead. It was not the most inspiring 90 minutes but with the score level at 1-1 there was to be extra-time and the real drama was to follow. With the temperatures plunging, I was seriously considering taking the kids home but the lure of more Scottish Cup glory was too strong. As we waited for extra-time to start, snow began to fall heavily and the referee insisted on the lines being swept before play could continue. There was a great deal of consultation going on between the match officials and representatives of both clubs but the decision was made to carry on. No more goals during extra-time and it all came down to penalties. It's funny how, in this situation, the hypothermia disappears and is replaced by an adrenalin rush and the warm feeling of expectation. It turned out to be another great victory over Premier League opposition as Ayr won 7-6 on penalties.

Our team seemed to be on the crest of a wave in terms of their Scottish Cup exploits but the League form was pretty poor. When we went to Motherwell for the Scottish Cup fourth round tie, I believed we had a wee chance and it turned out to be another great away day with Ayr winning, thanks in part to a great vocal backing from a large travelling support. By this time, Madeleine was taking a keen interest in anything Ayr United and she had found a hero in Glynn Hurst, who was leading the Ayr United line and scoring goals on a regular basis. We were treated to a goals feast and a great display of attacking football from the 'Honest Men'. In a first half packed with goalmouth action, Ayr opened the scoring when Gary Teale met a Mickey Reynolds cross on the half volley to slam it past Andy Goram. The roar that went up from the Ayr supporters must have given the players an almighty lift but the pressure grew on the team when an injury to Craig Nelson in the Ayr goal meant that he had to leave the field to receive stitches in a leg wound and meanwhile John Robertson kept goal in a frantic seven minutes. I was mightily relieved at the sight of 'Nelly' returning to the pitch just ahead of a Motherwell corner but sod's law dictated that a few seconds later Motherwell would be awarded a goal. I choose my words carefully when using the word 'awarded' because the ball never crossed the line at any point. Lee McCulloch's header was blocked on the line before being booted up the park. It was fury that greeted the referee's decision and I for one was screaming my head off at the injustice of the goal award. The referee, Martin Clark, could only have guessed that the ball had crossed the line but like it or not, we were level again. My anger was magnified when Motherwell went ahead. Don Goodman slid in to force the ball home and all of a sudden we were behind. It was not exactly doom and gloom at the Ayr end because the style of play adopted by this particular Ayr United team meant that they would definitely create more chances. They duly equalised when wee Mickey Reynolds raced into the 'Well penalty area and was barged off the ball. A confident Gary Teale stepped up and sent Andy Goram the wrong way from the penalty spot. A hundred yards away, at the opposite side of the ground, we were hugging, dancing, cheering and waving our black and white flags and scarves. The fifth goal of the first half went to Motherwell when Goodman fell over Craig Nelson's legs and the referee gave the penalty. I did not get a good view of the incident but there was no doubt in my mind...he dived. My 'boos' had no influence over the referee and Brannan slotted home the kick. I had already settled for a one-goal deficit at half-time but Craig Nelson's decision to punt the ball almost the full length of the park brought Ayr their third goal with a completely hysterical reaction from the travelling fans. Glynn Hurst, with his back to goal controlled the long kick perfectly and when he guided the ball to Neil Tarrant, a loan player from Aston Villa, the big fellow unleashed a perfect left foot drive to beat Goram at his left hand post. Five minutes after the game had started it was half-time, or so it seemed. It had been one of those games that flew past. In the chat I had with everyone around me during the interval, I had no recollection of the goal times, I had to be reminded of the goalscorers and I even had to check if the score was indeed 3-3. It had been an exhilarating experience, six goals and Ayr fighting back twice. When the teams reappeared for the second half, an almighty roar erupted from the Ayr support. We were prepared for another exciting 45 minutes, knowing that Ayr would go for it with speed merchants like Teale, Hurst and Reynolds capable of causing panic in the Premier League team's defence with their positive attacking style. Tarrant's undoubted ability as a striker was confirmed when he tucked away his chance to win the game for Ayr after his great team work with Hurst and Teale. Yesssss! A fourth goal from our heroes and this time, right in front of our eyes. Forgetting my 45 years, like a teenager, I was off, down the steps and then back up the steps, stopping briefly to hug strangers on my way. Thankfully, the goal glut ended there and we were going to be in the fifth round draw. The only down-side on the day was the sending off of Mickey Reynolds. Motherwell had brought on Pat Nevin as a substitute and wee Mickey was guilty of a rash challenge on Nevin to pick up his second yellow card. All things considered though, it had been a fantastic, albeit draining, experience.

Where there had been very little pressure as underdogs in previous Scottish Cup matches, Ayr were expected to take care of Partick Thistle in the quarter-final of the competition. The home draw was an extra advantage and although the game was very nervy, Ayr managed a 2-0 win to go through to the semi-final of the Scottish Cup.

My recollection of those heady days against Celtic in the Scottish League Cup semi-final in 1969 and against Rangers in the 1973 Scottish Cup semi-final came flooding back and I had this euphoric anticipation of glory being imminent. On 8 April 2000 our whole family travelled up to Hampden Park. We joined together with a large group of our friends and another 10,000 Ayr United fans, dreaming of history being made. From the guys in their black and white cow outfits, to the masses in jester hats with jingling bells, thousands of fans with current replica strips and also jerseys from years gone by. Unfortunately, it all ended in tears and a 7-0 thrashing from Rangers. Madeleine, Simon and I still felt committed to attending the after match celebration arranged for Ayr supporters at the Centrum in Prestwick Toll. It was more like a wake, albeit with a couple of shreds of consolation. One being that Madeleine had her photograph taken with Glynn Hurst, her hero and the other that Simon managed to acquire an autographed pair of goalie gloves from Marius Rovde, Ayr's Icelandic goalkeeper. In typical fashion, Simon had to take the Mickey and he ridiculed the poor guy, who had no idea what Simon was talking about. As my toes curled with embarrassment, Simon then proceeded to ask Marius for his gloves as a memento and the big goalkeeper duly obliged after penning his autograph on them.

The relative Scottish Cup success the club had enjoyed in the previous few years was not replicated in 2001. Madeleine, Simon and I had decided to travel to Inverness for the third round tie with Inverness Caledonian Thistle and at our 8am departure time off we went on our five-hour journey. We arrived at the ground in good spirits and full of optimism about our chances of progressing to the fourth round and by half-time our thoughts had already turned to who we might draw in the next round. That may seem a tad presumptuous but we were leading 3-0. Simon's joy was unbridled after the third goal and he had good reason to be excited come half-time. 'My bet is up already and it's only half-time,' said Simon. On the Friday he had gone into William Hill the bookmakers in Ayr and placed a bet on Ayr to win 3-0. His £5 stake at odds of 25/1 meant that he would collect £130 on Monday morning. He waved his betting slip around and told anyone who would listen how insightful he had been. I did point out that there was a small matter of the second half still to negotiate before his dispensable income was boosted. 'Don't worry about it,' said the bold Simon. 'I had a funny feeling in the pit of my stomach, I knew it would be 3-0 today.' I didn't want to spoil his party but I suggested that it might have been a touch of wind that had caused the funny feeling. By the end of the match, every Ayr supporter had more of a sinking feeling in his or her stomach. The transformation in Ayr United's fortunes that day was remarkable. Not that luck played a part. Ayr United capitulated in the second half. Before Inverness had pulled one back I had remarked to Madeleine and Simon that Ayr looked exposed through the middle and though I hate to say it, I was proved correct. Simon was still congratulating himself about his result forecasting and would hear nothing of my doom and gloom prediction that the game was not over yet. Inverness scored and then piled pressure on the Ayr defence with raid after raid. 'This doesn't look good. I think we're in trouble here,' I said. Simon was cursing his luck by now, 'My bet's down, how unlucky is that?' Madeleine pointed out that Ayr seemed to have decided to play the second half in all out defence. 'Why did they not just continue playing the same way?' she asked. Why indeed. If the writing was not already on the wall when Inverness scored their second goal, Gordon Dalziel hammered the last nail in the coffin, to use another cliché, by substituting Gary Teale with a defender straight after the score had been reduced to 3-2. Ayr's travelling support was totally bemused by the substitution, as it appeared that Teale was not injured in any way. Confirmation of that fact came from Gary Teale himself, as he walked sullenly towards the away bench, shaking his head in disbelief. I may not have been particularly enamoured by Teale as a player but it seemed to me that on the day he was the one player who could take some of the pressure off the Ayr defence by taking the ball for a run up the wing and generally holding onto possession. Gordon Dalziel thought differently. If someone had offered us a draw at that very moment, I would have taken it with delight. It seemed like it would only be a matter of time before Inverness would equalise and then go on to win the match. That is exactly what happened.

Half-time:
Inverness Caledonian Thistle 0 Ayr United 3.
Full time:
Inverness Caledonian Thistle 4 Ayr United 3.

With the Scottish Cup dream over for another year, Ayr managed to finish a creditable second in their First Division campaign but the desire of an Ayr supporter to return to the Premier League was frustrated by Livingston who ended the campaign with a seven point cushion. Our expectations were such that finishing second seemed at that time like abysmal failure.

We're All Going to Hampden

In the 2001-02 season, my club were trying in vain to escape the confines of the First Division but the Cup runs were certainly providing lots of excitement. The tail end of 2001 saw the beginning of Ayr's CIS Cup campaign and when the second round draw matched us with Stranraer, it signalled the start of a cup run that would go down as the most successful in the club's history. A 4-0 victory set Ayr up for yet another Cup-tie with Kilmarnock. The home tie on 9 October attracted a crowd of over 7,000 and we were ready for another night of high drama. Our lads were not going to disappoint us.

Ayr had made a promising start but, to be honest, the prospects looked bleak after 40 minutes when Paul Sheerin was sent off. Nevertheless, the team hung in to soak up the pressure exerted by the Premier League team for the remaining five minutes of the first period and the entire second half of the match. With the advantage of the extra man, Kilmarnock still could not find the breakthrough and Ayr forced the match into a penalty shoot out, despite being under the cosh for the majority of the game. Craig Nelson had one of those nights when nothing was getting past him. Ayr United had earned the opportunity to progress to the quarter-final and their five kicks from the spot would decide it. The match itself may not have been the most enthralling but the penalty shoot-out was to provide us with a roller-coaster ride of emotional excitement that would be etched in the memory for a long time to come. The Somerset Road end of the ground was the setting for the drama about to unfold. I was beside myself with nerves as the teams selected the five players who would be faced with the unenviable task of dealing with the pressure associated with a shot from 12 yards out. My stomach sank when wee Brian McLaughlin had his shot saved by Gordon Marshall. He may have been ridiculed for that famous Andy Walker chipped penalty in 1999 but Marshall was an excellent goalkeeper. It looked like a lost cause but Craig Nelson continued his heroics with a great save from Craig Dargo. Maybe we could still pull it off. The noise from the Ayr crowd reached a new height when Chris Innes inexplicably mishit his shot and the packed crowd surged forward in anticipation as Neil Duffy stepped up with a chance to take Ayr through at the expense of our esteemed neighbours. By this time I was oozing confidence and I was certain the big man would finish the job. He appeared nerveless as he stroked the ball into the back of the net and Somerset Park went wild. Cue the hugs for my daughter and the woman on the other side of me. 'We did it mister,' screamed the wee boy who had attached himself to me and I think it was his dad who then joined us in a three-man jig conducted in a square foot of the terracing. As the crowd left the ground, I was on top of the world. We had been virtually down and out but the 'Honest Men' turned it around and grabbed their victory against all the odds.

I arrived home and my agitated condition would not allow me to relax. I was in a heightened state of euphoria and, feeling that I had to do something, I sat at the computer and typed out a limerick, of a very low standard I admit, to acknowledge the heroes of another great Ayr United victory. The title reflected on the achievement of our cup successes against our old enemies; 'FOUR IN A ROW'. Our recent record showed a nice progressive pattern too;

13/8/96: Kilmarnock 0 Ayr United 1
14/2/98: Ayr United 2 Kilmarnock 0
23/1/99: Ayr United 3 Kilmarnock 0

OK, so this time round it was a 0-0 draw after extra-time but a glorious penalty shoot out victory had made it four wins from four Cup ties. On the night of this latest triumph I had laughed when I eavesdropped on a conversation between a couple of pals on the terracing, before the match had started. 'Tam, see how we've beat them three times in a row? If we beat them tonight, do we get to keep them?' The answer was matter of fact 'Aye, I think we do Wullie'.

I sent my little verse to every one of my Kilmarnock acquaintances and delighted in their gloom.

FOUR IN A ROW

It's rarely fun coming to Ayr
For Killie it's so hard to bear
Although they do try
They feel like a cry
When they leave feeling battered and 'sair'

The blues find it so hard to score
Their play is described as a bore
While Ayr push up front
Killie take all the brunt
Ayr fans ask, is it going to be four?

But alas the score-sheet stays blank
Ayr have Craig Nelson to thank
The ref sends off Sheerin
With Killie fans cheerin'
A decision that Ayr fans think rank

Extra-time looms with great tension
Ten-man Ayr feel great apprehension
They scrap like survivors
As McLaren leads the divers
Can't pass Hughes, though he's on a pension

No breakthrough, it's penalty kicks
This is better than the Odeon flicks
The atmosphere's dense

The players are tense
And the Ayr fans give it big licks

It's at this stage that all does seem lost
Marshall saving the ball down at his post
McLaughlin's wee flick
Just wasn't the trick
And it looks like there will be great cost

But wait Nelson saves, it's not finished
Ayr fans thought their chance had diminished
But Dargo has failed
As Nelson is hailed
The Rugby Park team are astonished

Big Duffer steps up with conviction
Knowing his side face extinction
A miss from Chris Innes
Was he on the Guinness?
Big Neil's won it, a great execution

Ayr then took their revenge for the previous year's Scottish Cup defeat by Inverness Caledonian Thistle by knocking out the Highlanders in the quarter-final. Admittedly, Ayr carried a lot of luck in the match and the result flattered us but the 5-1 victory was just what we needed to forget about the 4-3 cup catastrophe in Inverness. At the start of 2002, Ayr began their Scottish Cup campaign with a 6-0 win at Deveronvale and for the rest of the season we had a great time. We never imagined for one moment that we would contest a Cup Final and also a Cup semi-final but that is what our wee club achieved. Our League form was not terrific but for excitement, the cup games never failed to get us going. The two major matches of the season were against the Old Firm.

After beating Hibernian 1-0 at Hampden Park in the semi-final of the CIS Cup, my voice disappeared for a couple of days. I shouted myself hoarse throughout the last 15 minutes of extra-time and the one word I constantly repeated was 'AWAY'. With Ayr ahead from an Eddie Annand penalty, expertly taken by the way, Hibs laid siege to the Ayr goal. A couple of crosses came into the Ayr 'box' and I shouted 'AWAY' both times to great effect as the Ayr defenders cleared their lines. At the time, I had the misguided belief that I was in some way responsible for keeping the ball out of the net with my timely roar. It stood to reason therefore, that if I continued shouting it when Hibs threatened, I would surely prevent a goal and help carry my team through to the Final. My inability to speak for a couple of days was well worth it. The crowd at the match was a poor 12,000 and although that was very disappointing, the tension and excitement involved, coupled with the best ever opportunity to reach a major Final, made it a night to remember. By this time, Madeleine, Simon, David and I were joined by the rest of my family and lots of friends. Although it was an expensive season, it was money well spent. We did it and with one Cup Final place successfully negotiated, we believed that there was every chance that Ayr could double up in cup glory. The team had been immense in the Scottish Cup and Dunfermline and Dundee United were brushed aside to set up a Scottish Cup semi-final against Celtic. A whirlwind six days in March 2002 saw Ayr lose 4-0 to Rangers in the CIS Cup Final before losing 3-0 to Celtic in the Scottish Cup semi-final the following weekend. Our day in the sunshine at Hampden Park for the CIS Cup Final was preceded by a sleepless night ahead of all the preparation for our trip to Glasgow. The hats and scarves had been purchased, the black and white beach balls had been blown up, our kids wore their face paint with pride and we joined the convoy north to do battle. Ayr had started the Final brightly and what I could only describe as a wonder save from Stefan Kloss, the Rangers goalkeeper, saved the blue half of the Old Firm from a terrible beating that day. If that ball had gone in, Ayr would have won the game by five or six goals. Unfortunately, the 'keeper somehow managed to keep out Brian McLaughlin's shot and Rangers went on to win the match 4-0. You'll perhaps have detected that I allowed myself a bit of latitude in using my imagination to describe what would have happened if…It is something you are allowed to do if you are an Ayr United fan. By 4.45pm our dreams had been shattered. I walked off and sat on my own with my head bowed, feeling sorry for myself, as the trophy was presented to Rangers. My wife came over and said 'Oh well, it's all over, they tried their best and that's all you can ask of them…let's go home'. As I stood up, she asked, 'Are you alright?' 'I'm fine,' I answered, 'I think I've got something in my eye'. The tears were flowing and although I was able to use my scarf to partly cover my face, I could not hide the fact that I was distraught. I had genuinely believed that it was going to be our day.

My depression lasted for a couple of days but there was no time to dwell on the disappointment. It was time to get excited about the Celtic semi-final. There were no tears after that match, despite the fact that we lost 3-0. Maybe it was because I was, by then, battle hardened and able to take defeat like a man. No, I finally understood that against either side of the Old Firm, we were always going to be up against it and we could only give it a go. Ayr certainly did give it a go that evening. Some guy called Larsson and another pain in the neck free kick expert called Thompson spoiled our fun but if anything, Ayr had played better than they did in the Cup Final the Sunday before. I felt really proud of my wee team that season. Over the years, I have tried in vain to explain to Rangers and Celtic supporters what it is like to support a team like Ayr United. We have never won anything of note but Ayr are my team and I support them through good times and bad times. We do not win trophies and we do not play in Europe but our relative success means as much to me as it does to Celtic or Rangers supporters when they win the League or Cup or enjoy an extended run in the UEFA Cup or whatever. I would regard a decent Cup run for Ayr United as on a par with Celtic or Rangers pitting their strengths against the cream of Europe in the Champions League. They will never win it but they are always prepared to give it their best shot. Actually, I am maybe being kind to the Old Firm as Ayr United might have a wee outside chance of winning the Scottish Cup one day, whereas I seriously doubt whether Rangers or Celtic will ever win another European trophy in my lifetime.

My darling daughter left home for University in October of that exciting year and we saw less of her as she moved first of all to Stirling University and then transferred to Strathclyde University in Glasgow as she developed her French and Spanish language skills. Her only exposure to Ayr United at the time was the occasional match when she was home for a weekend, listening to my moans and looking for the results from afar. I may have felt bereft at the thought of my football buddy deserting me for education but as parents, my wife and I did not handle her departure from home very well at all. Nicholas, our eldest, had moved to Glasgow a couple of years before and although it was a disappointment that he was not around as much, we were confident in his ability to take on his independence and be successful. Madeleine, on the other hand, was determined to leave school after fifth year and go to university early.

We Are The Champions

In another big event of 2002, I crossed swords again with my old adversary, Billy Walker, the Cumnock Juniors manager. This time the competition was the Miners' Welfare Tournament, held at Loch Park, New Cumnock in July. The tourney was popular with teams from all over the West of Scotland and I entered the Valspar team with the expectation of a good day out for everyone. The setting of the Junior's football stadium was ideal. It was a one day tournament which necessitated a 9am start and for those teams who negotiated their way to the latter stages of the tourney, they could expect to be playing till 6pm, a long day for 10-year-old kids but they loved it. We had enjoyed playing in the previous year's tournament and as soon as we received the invitation for the 2002 competition I had responded by sending back the entry form the same day.

The previous year's competition had been greatly enjoyed by our players, despite the fact that the team was knocked out at the quarter-final stage. We had been short of players for that tournament, for one reason or another, but thanks to a late phone call to a friend of my nephew Douglas, a youngster from Troon Juniors football club helped out by joining us as a 'guest' for the day. Young Jamie Ness slotted into the team perfectly. We had some really nice players in our team but to be honest, this boy was a cut above. Nevertheless, I gave him the same amount of time on the park as the other players in the squad. The same player developed in leaps and bounds in the years ahead. He went on to play outstandingly for Ayr Boswell Boys Club in his youth and he went on to show that he is now one of the top young players in the country, playing for Glasgow Rangers before joining Stoke City. Once it had become obvious that Jamie would carve out a career in professional football, I did get the chance to explain to his dad that his success was probably due to the one day he spent with Valspar 1991s and my incredible coaching. Seriously though, it is a pleasure seeing a local boy achieve a dream of making it to the top and what a well-mannered, respectful and pleasant boy I found him to be.

My 2002 tournament squad would have been so much stronger for the presence of Jamie but I never made the call. It was only right to stick with the 12 players who were registered with the club and we would win or lose with these kids. Our players enjoyed a good run of form during the day and played their way through to the quarter-final where they won 2-0 against Billy Walker's Cumnock Juniors. He was the first to congratulate us and wish us the best of luck for the remainder of the tournament. As it happened, we may have had the upper hand over Cumnock Juniors in this tournament and perhaps throughout the seven-a-side development years but when the full-sided matches were introduced at age 12, Billy's team developed into a much better side than ours.

In 2004, I was shocked to hear that Billy had died suddenly, at the age of 37, and I felt compelled to attend his funeral in Cumnock to pay my respects. The rain was torrential and the cloud-filled sky matched my mood. We would need to do without a positive contributor to local youth football development and over and above the heartache endured by his family and friends; I knew that Ayrshire youth football had lost one of the good guys.

The semi-final went our way as we experienced the type of luck that is required by any team at any level to reach the latter stages of tournaments. The first half had been goalless and our opponents, Kyle Boys Club pounded away at our goal for the entire second half. Just as it seemed that extra-time would need to be played, the ball fell to 'Pagey' David Page was our wee star striker who was a natural goalscorer with a good turn of speed but he was completely out on his feet by this time. Why he was standing a yard inside the opposition half, instead of being in the front line of our attack, I will never know but instead of going for a run with the ball or trying to find a pass, he launched the ball forward and to the amazement of everyone watching, it sailed over the goalkeeper's head and into the net. 1-0 Valspar. The kids held on for a couple of minutes more to record the win that took them into the Tournament Final. The players found enough energy to jump up and down, embrace one another and shout and scream in delight but in contrast, the Kyle team were inconsolable. They had been the better team throughout the match but had lost to a freak goal in the dying minutes of the match.

The focus then turned to the other semi-final, which was still to finish. This was the match that was likely to produce the tournament winners. Ayr Boswell FC faced Bellfield Royals. I would have expected the Ayr team to edge a close match but when I asked a spectator how the game was going, I was shocked to learn that the Kilmarnock team were 6-0 ahead. The game ended seconds later and we then knew that the Final would be contested between Bellfield Royals and Valspar FC.

The Bellfield players were already behaving as if they were tournament champions. They were winding our boys up, making wild predictions about the score in the Final and how the cup was theirs. The Valspar players sat quietly and never responded. They believed that they had no chance. I had no reason to think that our boys could pull off the biggest victory of all but I went through the motions and, along with everyone who had supported the team throughout what was a long, energy sapping day, we tried to motivate the players for one last effort. The Bellfield coaches and parents were very generous in their praise of our team getting to the Final, to the point of being patronising in fact. Nevertheless, we exchanged, 'May the best team win,' comments along with handshakes and smiles. There was a time gap to allow both teams some rest before the Final and as a result, the match kicked off at 6pm.

The large crowd of parents on each side of the pitch added to the atmosphere and the euphoria on the Bellfield touchline seemed to be a precursor to the celebrations awaiting them once Valspar had been disposed of. The opening exchanges were a delight for me as our kids had found a new lease of life. 'Pagey' brought out a good save from the opposition 'keeper and Ben sent a low drive just wide of the post. The Bellfield supporters were not amused and they let their players know about it. Ten minutes in and our team were awarded a free kick about 15 yards from goal. Jay Ritchie stepped up and sent the ball screaming high into the Bellfield net with a powerful drive. Our boys were 1-0 up in the Final. For the remainder of the half, Valspar defended stoutly as Bellfield stepped up the pressure. Jordan Hood pulled off some wonderful saves and the lead remained intact at the half-time break. I must concede that Valspar were subjected to an onslaught in the second period and I could not see how our boys could hold out. They were doing anything they could to prevent the other team scoring. Closing down their opponents, blocking shots and making last ditch tackles. In one such tackle, Neil Bonsor took a sore kick on his ankle and the referee waved me on to check out his injury. He was in pain and crying and it was obvious that he could not continue. As I tried to console him, the crowd on the Bellfield touchline were shouting and swearing at the referee, insisting that the player should be taken off the park so the game could be restarted. I picked Neil up and carried him towards our touchline, to the background sound of the opposition supporters cursing and swearing because I never took him off their side, as it was closer. They showed no concern for the 10-year-old who had been hurt and really let themselves down with their behaviour. As I walked off with Neil, I turned and shouted in their general direction, 'If you need the trophy that badly, just take it'. Their coach replied that I was, 'out of order'. Yep, I was out of order and his group of spectators were entitled to shout foul mouthed obscenities because I was attending to the well being of a 10-year-old. The logic of some people in a football environment can sometimes evaporate as emotions take over. The Bellfield players copied the aggression from the touchline and the resultant free kicks they conceded allowed Valspar some respite and the final whistle blew to the relief and sheer delight of everyone associated with our club.

The Bellfield coaches grudgingly shook hands with me at the end and the parents and associates on the opposite touchline from us continued their foul-mouthed rants. The Kilmarnock youngsters took the lead from their adult mentors and refused to shake hands with our players. It was all quite distasteful. In amongst the celebrations, some of the Valspar parents complained to me about the conduct of the Bellfield people but worse behaviour was to follow. As the organisers set up a table in readiness for the presentation of the trophy and medals, I congratulated our players individually and thanked them for their efforts throughout a very long day. The players from both teams then lined up and the Tournament Director gave a short speech praising both teams for producing an excellent display of football to grace the Final. He then congratulated the Bellfield team on playing so well and finishing as runners-up before asking their players to go up to collect their medals. The traditional shaking of hands and handing over of the boxed medals took place and it was now the turn of Valspar to be commended by the Tournament Director for achieving the status of Tournament Champions. As the gentleman waxed lyrical about the performance of our team, the Bellfield coach gathered his players and they and their supporters left Loch Park before the trophy and medals were presented to our players. The Bellfield contingent had blotted their copybook again and embarrassed their club by their conduct. It had never been in the script for Valspar to reach the Final, far less win the match and the response from everyone connected to the other team was undignified, to say the least. Having arrived in New Cumnock at quarter to nine in the morning, here we were, over 10 hours later, finally at the end of the tournament. It is tantamount to child abuse but I am sure that the same kids who took part look back at that day with fond memories. Jay Ritchie stepped up, as Captain of the team, to collect the large silver cup and as he held it aloft the players jumped up and down, with renewed energy, in celebration of their great victory. Coca Cola was poured into the trophy and each of the players took their turn in lifting the cup and toasting their success.

It was to be the one and only time the team won a trophy during the 11 years the team was in existence but, to draw comparisons with my heroes at Ayr United, my association with the club was not just about winning. I had always been interested in the community aspect of the club. I wanted everyone to feel affiliated to Valspar Football Club and for all the kids to develop values as well as skills. Before long our team were embarking on their journey in competitive football and after some serious fundraising we generated enough money to take the kids to their first 11-a-side football tournament in Blackpool in 2003. Despite the poor weather and disappointing results, the social bonding that took place was very positive and the highlight of the tournament was in our last match. We were drawn against a team from Northern Ireland in the semi-final of the 'Plate' (the consolation section of the tournament for teams who failed to qualify to the knockout stages of the main event). In a very close match, our team lost 1-0 and when the final whistle was blown, the winning team teased our kids, calling them names and generally gloating. Our boys were particularly angry but before they got involved in a fight, I gathered them all in a group and gave them an opportunity to take the moral high ground. I explained that by going over to the other team, shaking their hands and wishing them the best of luck in the Final, they would be the 'bigger' team. It was quite amusing for our group of parents to watch as the boys approached the opposition players. The Irish boys stood up in anticipation of a confrontation and when the Valspar players offered handshakes and best wishes, they were dumbfounded. The Irish team responded to the magnanimous gesture, instantly dropping their aggressive attitude and instead commiserated with our players. I was very proud of the kids and I think they were pleased with themselves too.

Next up was the serious business of competitive league football and in August 2003, we embarked on our journey in the West of Scotland League. Despite starting off with a 7-5 victory at home to Tass Thistle, the team had a mediocre season and eventually finished sixth in the league. Our team were never going to be world-beaters but they were a decent bunch of kids who enjoyed their football. Valspar Football Club had been a vibrant club since Jim Gourlay established it back in 1976. By 2003 however, the number of teams representing Valspar had dwindled. As teams reached age 19 level they played their final year of youth football and the gap that was created by that team folding was naturally filled by the team at the age group below. The problem was that in the recent years a couple of teams had folded prematurely and the gaps were growing. Davy Agnew and Lee Dodds were two of the team managers who had successful teams in the 1988 and 1989 age groups respectively and when they were approached by Campbell Money, who was responsible for youth development at Ayr United, Valspar lost another two teams as they jumped ship to form two new age group teams representing Ayr United. At that time, I was standing on the terraces at each home game, listening to conversation among Ayr fans praising Money for the excellent work he was doing in developing youngsters at the club. I do not have any depth of knowledge about the youth development at Ayr United at that time but I do know that he took Davy's team, with a long unbeaten run in any competition, and changed their team name from Valspar to Ayr United overnight. He then did the same with Lee's team. Sorry, but that is not youth development. It was cherry picking to acquire successful teams that he was then able to take credit for.

A few years later and Valspar consisted of only three teams. It looked like the club was on the way out. I joined together with my colleagues, Jim Clark and Brian Graham and we hatched a plan to revive the club. We requested a meeting with the committee of the club and presented our plan. It involved a new constitution, code of conduct, managers' guidelines and a raft of formalities to re-structure the club as well as an idea to introduce a 'Junior' section to recruit youngsters from the age of five, with the intention of developing basic football skills before establishing teams to enter seven-a-side league football in the years ahead. Our ideas to revitalise the club were accepted and at the Annual General Meeting, I was elected as chairman of the Club. Along with Brian and Jim, I had big ideas to transform Valspar from a club with disparate teams using the same name, to a community club with pride and values. Winning matches would remain a priority but developing every club member's individual skills as well as instilling community values would be of equal importance.

I am not sure how I pulled it off but I talked my wife into taking on the role of manager-coach of the 'Juniors' section of the club. Our aim was to create a thriving community club with teams at every age group and Marilyn obtained her coaching certificate and took on the responsibility of developing the basic skills of our youngest members. Marilyn's keen interest in football, along with her sporting background as a netball player who represented Scotland in her younger years, stood her in good stead as she made a positive impact in bringing on the footballers of the future. As the numbers grew in her section, Marilyn recruited her friend, Karlene Mackie, and they developed and prepared teams, from their base in Queen Margaret Academy, for their introduction to seven-a-side football at age seven. The next two years went really well and the 'Juniors' coaches established teams to represent Valspar and so trigger the recovery of the parent club.

Down Somerset Park way, the Bill Barr money had dried up and the thrills and spills of the cup runs were never likely to be repeated in the near future. 2002-03 was to result in a sixth place finish in the First Division and early exits in all the cup competitions. The period that followed was probably the most inauspicious in the club's history. Campbell Money, Mark Shanks, the 'Two Rabs', Robert (Bobby) Connor and Robert Reilly and then Neil Watt all had a go at reviving the club's fortunes between 2002 and 2007. It is easy to criticise any, or all, of the above but to be fair they had very little to work with at a club that appeared to be sailing close to the wind, in financial terms. During those dark years, the talk around the town was that Ayr United could go out of business altogether. The gloom and doom that descended on the town was exacerbated by the news of the death of Ally MacLeod on 1 February 2004. The passing of our leader saddened the whole town of Ayr. He was certainly like no other, in terms of giving us, players and fans alike, the belief that we really could achieve great things. In an interview with Alex Cameron of the *Daily Record* back in 1969, with Ayr sitting at the top of the First Division, a quote the paper attributed to the Ayr United manager read, '…there is a long way to go yet…and there is sure to be a levelling out process. But some of us will hold on'. He had convinced me, and probably everyone associated with the club, that we could win the league. When one considers that his comments came one month into a new season and referred to a part-time team competing with the best teams Scotland had to offer, it illustrates just how charismatic our leader was. I have learned from my experience following Ayr United that supporters of provincial clubs need nothing more than…hope. The probability of our team winning a major honour in my lifetime may well be remote but as long as we believe there is the slightest chance, our optimism will sustain us. Ally MacLeod instilled in us, the belief that anything is possible and in that context he was irreplaceable. Perhaps those of us who supported Ayr United in the 1960s and 1970s are unrealistic in our expectations of our current team but MacLeod achieved his successes with his motivational qualities, not with cash. We can bemoan the lack of resources available to our club but the late, great Ally MacLeod proved that with the right man at the helm, money is not everything. He managed to get the best out of his players and filled them with the confidence that meant they feared nobody. Seemingly mediocre players became giants on the park and the main beneficiaries were the Ayr United fans. Given a choice between a manager with great coaching ability and tactical awareness, and one who can motivate players to perform at their peak, I would take the charismatic motivator every time. The question is, where do we find another Ally?

The pull of Ayr United during the early years of the 21st century was not exactly magnetic. If the truth be told, it was only my allegiance and perceived obligation as a supporter that kept me going to matches. There was very little in the way of entertainment being served up and I would describe this period as an all time low in all the years I have supported the club. I was returning home from matches swearing that I would not be back. I returned for each home match hoping for a sudden upturn in our fortunes but there was no quick fix. We had gone from the dizzy heights of a Cup Final, to regular defeats by teams we would not have taken seriously a few years earlier.

World Cup Football

The despondency I was feeling as an 'Honest Man' was not dampening my enthusiasm and commitment to Valspar Football Club. After our team's debut season in competitive football, I called a meeting of the parents to suggest a trip for the team to a tournament abroad and I provided details of events in Spain, Denmark and Sweden. After some deliberation and discussion about how to raise the finances for such a trip, we decided to aim for the Gothia Cup in Sweden. The Gothia Cup, held in Gothenburg, is well known in youth football circles as the premier youth football tournament in the world and I was sure that the boys would experience something that would become a long lasting positive memory of their youth football days. I held a fundraising meeting for all the parents and we organised a series of events to generate finance to offset the costs of the trip. Our players were holding their own on the football field as we were joined by a few more additions to our squad. One of these recruits was a young Ross Robertson who performed particularly well for us in that season. Of all the players that were registered with the Valspar 1991 team, a few went on to join the youth ranks at senior football clubs but the biggest success story has been Ross. It is nice to see any of my ex-players doing well and I was particularly pleased when Ross made the breakthrough into the Ayr United team. He contributed well in his midfield role for Valspar football club and he's now wearing the famous black and white and living my boyhood dream.

Generating funds for our Gothia Cup trip was a big undertaking but everyone rallied round to put on race nights, sponsored walks, bag packing in supermarkets etc. So, on Saturday 16 July 2005 we left with a party of 33 people from Prestwick Airport for a week in Sweden's second city. From the moment we touched down in the city of Gothenburg, the organisation was second to none. A coach was waiting to drive us to our accommodation and within an hour of arriving in Gothenburg, we were being assisted by helpful staff in the school that had been commandeered for our accommodation, alongside another six or seven clubs. Our bedroom was a general classroom on the ground floor. We were able to collect our camp beds from a central point and we lined the perimeter of the classroom with 20 beds, side by side. Once we added the luggage and team kit bags to the space, there was not a lot of room left for manoeuvre. Four adults and 16 children holed up in one room for a week. The boys loved it but I have to say, it was not as appealing to me, Brian Graham, Jim Clark and Sandy Lawrie. We were 'slumming' it while the remainder of our adult party were accommodated in a smart hotel a mile up the road. One of the biggest advantages of staying in the school was that the four supervisors were in the same room as the players and we were able to keep an eye on the boys to ensure that they were safe and behaving responsibly. The added benefits included the interaction with the other squads who shared the school with us. Our boys mixed well with teams from Brazil, Uganda, Nigeria and America. In terms of the team's ability, we could have been described as mediocre at best and I just hoped that the team would cope with the standard of teams we may come up against. There were around 1,500 teams from all over the world playing at age groups from 12 to 19 years and I was under no illusion about progressing to the business end of the tournament. Nevertheless, I wanted the boys to play to their potential and make every game a contest. The social side would take care of itself and on the evening of our arrival, wee David Page emerged as the Valspar Ambassador. As soon as we were settled, we arranged to meet the parents at the main hub of activity, the Heden Centre which was a 10 minute walk from our school accommodation and equidistant from the hotel. As we walked down towards our meeting point, a group of players and coaches with bright green and red tracksuits were walking in the opposite direction on the other side of the road. I guessed that they were Africans. They were tall and slim, the epitome of top athletes. Without a word from anyone, 'Pagey' split from our group and headed across the road towards the other squad. I shouted after him to get back in our group but he was having none of it. He made a bee-line for a tall, gangly black guy who I guessed was around 20 years old and immediately struck up a conversation in his thick Ayrshire accent. He assumed that the other boy would understand him perfectly and as I rushed to his side fearing a diplomatic incident, he opened up with, 'Awright big man, where are you fae?' The big guy look perplexed. 'Pagey' put out his hand and his African counterpart shook it and smiled. 'Am fae Maybole, have ye heard ae it?' said Pagey. No response. Finally, another young man in their party took control. By this time, both squads of players were in one large group each curious to know more about the other. 'What is your name?' said the smaller, more confident boy. He had incredibly smooth, black skin, piercing brown eyes and a friendly smile. 'Pagey' reverted to best Sunday manners 'David, how? whit's yours?' 'Mugisa...' came the reply '...I'm from Uganda'. We found out later in the week that the boy's name meant 'lucky' but when you saw these boys play football, luck was something that was not required.

Every evening of the week that we were in Gothenburg, youngsters from all over the world congregated in the playground of the school to display their football skills and to try out their new tricks as they competed with one another. It was a pleasure watching our boys mix with Brazilians, Nigerians, Americans, Norwegians and Italians. I would have expected the language barriers to interfere with their communication but they all managed just fine using the universal language of football and hand gestures. In our tournament schedule, we were faced with three group matches in three days. The first of these was against an Italian team from Treviglio, near Milan. We travelled free on the Gothenburg train network to the Kungsbacka nine playing fields for our group matches. It was a large park with a dozen pitches in very good condition. The Italian team looked more like 18-year-olds than 14-year-olds and we were a shade apprehensive going into our first match. As it turned out, it was an evenly contested match eventually resulting in a 2-0 win to Treviglio. There was no time for the boys to feel sorry for themselves as that evening the opening ceremony was to be held. Ahead of our trip to Sweden we had all been excited about competing in the world's biggest youth football tournament but we never quite grasped the scale of the event until we arrived at the Ullevi Stadium for the opening ceremony. 45,120 packed out the stadium for the parade of competing countries and a variety of entertainment that thrilled us all. Rock bands, dancers, singers, drummers, fireworks and much more provided an adrenalin rush that set the boys up perfectly for the matches ahead and the only issue for us, as leaders, was how we could get the boys settled down for a good night's sleep before our second match at 9.30am the next morning. We tried reasoning and it failed. We then went for blackmail, 'Sleep or you're dropped'. That didn't work either. Threatening bodily harm seemed to do the trick but by that time it was 1.30am I will admit that there was a certain pleasure to be derived, at 7am, from tormenting the party animals from the night before with as much noise as possible. A quick breakfast before sprinting to catch the Kungsbacka train and before we knew it, our second match was underway. If ever there was a mismatch between two teams, this was it. The Swedish team, Hammarby IF 2, came with a good reputation and we were soon to discover that it was earned. They dominated the match from the first whistle and our boys were being overrun by bigger, stronger and more athletic players. After 20 minutes, and with our team 2-0 down and pinned back in our own box, Hammarby were awarded a free kick on the edge of our penalty area. I feared that number three was coming up. Worse was to follow. I was stunned to see the referee hold aloft a red card and it was for our captain, Jay Ritchie. We were two goals behind and our most influential player was standing on the touchline beside me. This was not going to end well. Jay claimed forcefully that he did nothing wrong and I made a mental note, 'speak to the referee at half-time'. We survived the free kick but lost a third goal before half-time. As Jim Clark dealt with the half-time talk to the players, I approached the referee. He was a 6ft 5in Swede, blonde-haired and as thin as a rake. I asked politely why Jay had been sent off and I reeled back in astonishment when he replied. Taking into consideration how well we had been treated by everyone since the moment we arrived in Gothenburg, I could not believe that a referee would speak to anyone in such a manner. He shouted loudly at me, 'FUCK OFF…' I was flabbergasted and indignant at the same time. 'He can't speak to me like that,' I thought to myself. It made no sense at all until finally, I realised that he had merely paused after these two very aggressive words to consider the use of his small amount of English before continuing '...HE SAID TO ME'. The meaning was a lot clearer now.

'FUCK OFF...HE SAID TO ME'.

Remonstrating with Jay was pointless, he denied it emphatically. When I relayed the story to the adults in our party that evening, everyone found it hysterically funny. It was less amusing that we eventually lost the match 8-0 and now we would be without our captain for match three, the next day. Balltorps FF, another Swedish club, were our opponents in the final group match and although we were not totally outplayed, we were comfortably beaten 4-0. The only game left for us now would be a knockout match in the 'B' tournament. There was no sense of despondency from the team. The boys had tried their best against good quality opposition and had come up short. On our arrival back at our school base, I gave the players some free time to wander around the shops and attractions at the Heden Centre while I went into our classroom to tidy the place up a bit. I sat on my camp bed, lay back and fell fast asleep. I was awakened some time later by a group of our players shouting loudly as they entered the room. Pulling myself together, I asked them what was wrong. The boys had been friendly with a party of American girls, Benson Soccer Girls from Oregon, who were on the third floor of our school accommodation and they had met up with them at the Heden Centre. On their way back to our school accommodation, as they approached the junction to cross over into the school grounds, one of the girls stepped into the road and into the path of a car. The boys had witnessed the car colliding with the 14-year-old girl and they were very shocked by it all. By the time we went outside, an ambulance had already left the scene of the accident with the girl who had apparently been badly hurt. The adults in our group managed to calm the boys down and we all waited anxiously for news of the young American girl. By 5pm we had heard nothing but the boys took matters into their own hands. They acquired a marker pen and laid their St Andrew's flag on the floor of our room. Each of the players then wrote on the flag, messages of support for the girl and when their task was complete they headed up to the room of the American team to deliver the flag. They had carried out their plan to show concern for the girl all on their own and the coaches of the girls team was glowing in his praise of the boys. When the news emerged the next morning, it was good. The young girl spent a night in hospital for observation and was then released, unscathed. The magnanimous nature of the US team saw them use some handicraft skills to create a number of 'friendship' bracelets made of beads and thread. They then presented one to each of our squad to thank them for their concern.

As our thoughts returned to the football, our hope was that we would be drawn against one of the weaker sides in the tournament whilst all of the other teams would be keen to be drawn against us. The team that we faced on the Thursday afternoon, with our tournament at stake, was Hauger FK from Norway. Our task was not nearly as onerous in comparison to the previous three matches. In a one-sided match, our boys played some nice football and created chance after chance without making the breakthrough. With five minutes left of normal time I sealed our fate by mentioning to Jim Clark that it would just be our luck to lose a late goal. The Norwegians had a rare foray into our half of the field and with the last action of the match, they bundled the ball home to win the match and send us crashing out of the tournament. Our adventure was over and the tears of the players were mainly due to frustration, as they had dominated the match. A trip to the amusement park that evening cheered everyone up and before we knew it we were back on our Ryanair flight home. On reflection, the decision to enter the team in the Gothia Cup was the right one. Despite the fact that the team had lost their four games without scoring a goal, I am certain that the players will remember their experience fondly and from what I observed they all thrived as young citizens, mixing well with young people from different countries. Although the feeling was that we were well short of the standards required for success at the tourney, our first opponents, Italian team Treviglio, went on to lift the trophy for the 'B' tournament, so maybe we were not as bad as we had imagined.

On our return to domestic youth league football we were hopeful of an upsurge in team spirit and confidence in the shape of progression of the team results but I was happy to give 'my boys' their chance to play football on a regular basis. It is natural for any parent to want the best for their children, so I can understand parents who wanted to see their sons play in the team all the time. I did try my best to make sure everyone in our squad got a chance to play, even if they were not the recognised 'superstars' of the club. On one such occasion, a father brought along his son, Callum, to one of our training nights and asked if he could join the club. The young boy was 5ft 10in tall and he was carrying around 14st in weight. His concerned dad believed that the training nights would contribute to the boy's fitness and help in his desire to lose weight. He had no expectation of his son being chosen for a match-day squad and told me as much. After a few weeks with us, I wanted to reward Callum for the hard work he put in. He was always last to complete any training task but he worked his socks off and never gave up. In the small-sided matches at the end of the training nights, he had virtually no mobility but he showed a really good touch on the ball. I made the decision to name him in the squad for a home match against Kilmarnock Balmoral on the following Saturday. When I told Callum and his dad that he would definitely play at some point in the match, I saw the shock in their faces followed by delight at the very prospect. Why shouldn't good lads like Callum be given a chance to enjoy football? He was never going to carve out a career for himself but then, how many of our kids make the grade?

We were struggling in the league, with only one team below us at the foot of the table. Kilmarnock Balmoral were a decent team who were at the opposite end of the table and they would expect to win comfortably against us. Sure enough, after 10 minutes of the second half, we were losing 4-0. With the game beyond us, I told Callum to warm up as he would be going on in midfield. The big fellow hurriedly discarded his tracksuit and stepped up to the touchline. I signalled to the referee that I wanted to make a substitution and on went big Callum, much to the amusement of the opposing players. He got an early touch of the ball and with it he started off a good move when he played an excellent pass out to our winger, Sean Clark. A minute later he beat his opponent to a header and the Balmoral player did not find it quite so funny. As I shouted encouragement to Callum, a figure appeared at my side. It was my old pal Brian Graham. His team was playing the next day, so he came down to see how things were going. Brian is a master of dry wit and he fired his question at me without the trace of a smile. 'Have you got the bus driver playing for you?' I justified my selection by raving about Callum 'This big guy's got a great touch and when he loses some weight, he'll do well. Look at that for a pass,' I said to him. 'There's a good player in there Brian', My wee mate was ready with a stinging riposte, 'Aye you're right, the bus driver must have swallied (swallowed) him'.

In my final season and a half running the 1991 team, our results were poor but the attitude among players and coaches was extremely positive. Alan Bonsor became a hate figure as he stretched the physical capacity of the boys with his fitness regime on training nights. The players only got down to ball work after hard exercise and long runs across the sand dunes of Ayr beach but they always had something left in the tank for the football drills. Alan always finished his stint in charge by shouting to the boys as he grinned, 'Right, that's the real work done, now it's playtime, they're all yours Gerry'. The man was a sadist and although the boys protested, they knew it made a positive impact on their fitness levels. There was always humour at training and at matches, whatever the score. On one occasion, we turned up for a match on a miserable day at the Old Racecourse but Jim Clark was in his usual happy-go-lucky mood. He also had a mischievous streak and on this day he had made several comments that had us all in stitches. Just before the match started, Jim pointed towards a group of our parents standing further down the touchline. 'That's some jacket Brian Dunlop's got on today,' said Jim. 'I'll bet you could see that thing from space,' Brian was wearing a luminous yellow, council work jacket. As the match got underway, Jim walked down the touchline and as he passed the group of parents, Brian, courteous as always, said, 'Morning Jim, how are you?' Jim turned, as if surprised by the comment and sharp as ever replied, 'Oh, hello Brian, I never saw you there.' Jim then proceeded to laugh at his own humour for the rest of the match. It's a good thing we had reasons to laugh because our results were poor. The boys were at an all-time low in terms of their confidence and we finished the season at the bottom of the league. We were not helped by ruthless individuals who poached our better players to bolster their teams. The coaches and managers of some of the more successful teams in our league had no qualms about weakening our team even further with their underhand dealings. It never seemed to bother them that they were breaking league rules in their pursuit of success. These people purport to foster the development of young footballers when in fact they are self-centred, inadequate and sad individuals who need to exploit young people for their own ends. There are plenty of these supposed altruists, who apparently give up their valuable time to organise youngsters, concerned only with the development of football skills of the boys in their charge. More accurately, they have little interest in the players they profess to support. I had no interest in recruiting 'better' players to replace the boys that I had. I wanted our players to be the best that they could be and my big hope was that I could play my part in rolling out that ethos within the parent club at Valspar. After 11 years, the team I had taken charge of on a temporary basis, for a couple of weeks, folded early in the 2006-07 season. Having started off the new campaign with heavy defeats, I was not prepared to put the boys through it anymore. I gathered the team together for a final night out and we spent the last few pounds we had on a 'last supper'. All good things come to an end.

In my capacity as chairman of the Valspar Football Club, I still had high hopes of helping to establish a community club with values that included more than just winning games. It took me a while to realise that the youth team managers at Valspar held a similar view to the ruthless individuals I had encountered during my time as manager of the 1991 team. By 2006, our plan to increase the number of teams had been successful and on the face of it, the club was thriving again. We had gone from three teams to 13 teams, thanks mainly to the Junior section of the club. Marilyn and Karlene were establishing a new team every year, ready to join the seven-a-side, non-competitive, West of Scotland League. My only concern was the attitude of newly recruited managers. At successive monthly meetings, the reports given at some age groups included criticism of the ability of some players. I was really uncomfortable with this and, as far as I was concerned, it was the responsibility of the coaches to develop the skills of members. When one coach gave his report, he alluded to the fact that some of his players were not good enough and he would be bringing in better players. The players he was coaching were nine years old. The coach of the team two years above this age group told us all that he was knocking on the doors of players registered with other clubs, to try and entice parents to bring their kids to Valspar. On the one occasion I challenged a coach, the response I received was that nobody would tell him how to run his team. Technically speaking, he was correct. The policy at the club, from the moment I joined in 1997, allowed each coach total autonomy in managing his team. The Life President of the club, Jim Gourlay, never questioned the approach taken by any of the coaches and I had no right to question them. Nevertheless, I was totally opposed to the 'win at all costs' style adopted by some of the coaches. No consideration was given to the children who were being replaced in their teams. Each of the coaches made a hollow remark about players being allowed to stay at the club for training only. These 'experts' were effectively dismissing the chances of young children to develop into good players. Their extensive knowledge as coaches was a year or two of running their own team, coupled with an 'Early Touches' coaching certificate. I may be wrong but rather than the exception to the rule, the situation at Valspar appears to be a microcosm of youth football in Scotland. No wonder Scottish football is failing. If youth coaches continue to make judgements about children before they have a chance to develop properly, children will have their potential dashed and be lost to the game. We all need to wake up to the reality that we are doing it all wrong at grass roots level. In this country, there appears to be a fixation with children who show up well at the very youngest ages while we neglect all others, seemingly oblivious to the possibility that children may develop at a later age. I approached some of the people at the club whom I felt would be sympathetic to my argument but I failed to garner enough support to instigate a debate on the philosophy and ethos of the club. I decided to resign as chairman of the club and, quite frankly, as I did not agree with the way things were evolving at Valspar, I decided to cut all my ties with the club. Marilyn and Karlene also severed their links with the club and handed in a healthy sum of money raised through subscriptions and fundraising by the Junior section of the club. At the next annual presentation of prizes, the club very kindly presented a glass plaque to Marilyn and me, to mark our contribution to the club over the years. So, our connection with Valspar Football Club came to an end, in a very amicable way.

The World of a Referee – It's a Riot

Walking away from my role as a chairman, manager, coach, administrator, and general dogsbody was a strange experience. For 10 years, I had spent most of my spare time involved in tasks associated with Valspar and now my leisure time was my own. Fundraising, club and league meetings, training sessions, telephone calls to managers, referees, parents and players, completing team lines, washing strips, keeping accounts and other associated tasks were all in the past.

With my training nights also finished, I was eager to stay active in some way and when I saw an advert in the paper for a referee-training course, I looked on it as an opportunity. If I managed to qualify as a ref, I could still be involved in the game and it would be a good way to maintain my level of fitness. 'Papa' Joe McGill, a referee well known by everyone involved in the local Ayrshire football scene, had often joked with me, 'You would make a great referee...well, you've been practising for all these years.' I made up my mind to enrol on the course organised by the Ayrshire Referees Association and in September 2006, I joined another 14 people at Grange Academy in Kilmarnock at the start of the 13-week course. On the first evening, I recognised some of the course trainers as referees who had officiated in matches from my amateur days and in my time coaching Valspar. We were all asked to introduce ourselves and to say why we wanted to become referees and, when it came to my turn, I described myself as a 'poacher turned gamekeeper'. I was alluding to the fact that I had spent years giving referees a hard time, as a player on the field and as a coach, from the touchline. The three regular trainers, along with the senior officials who dropped in from time to time, during the 13 weeks of the course, were very knowledgeable and also supportive. The result was that we all successfully passed the exam at the end of our training and we were now ready to take our first matches. I performed at an acceptable level, in the opinion of my supervisors and was then given 'probationary' status in the association.

Although I spent a relatively short time refereeing in the national sport, I discovered very quickly that there was a great deal of pleasure to be derived from officiating. I handled my first match as a referee in February 2007 and my four years as a referee was enough time for me to sample the good, the bad and the ugly side of football from a new perspective. My only regret is that I never started sooner. Although the pleasure and satisfaction I experienced as a referee could never compare to the excitement and pleasure I got from playing football at youth, amateur and pub league levels, as well as the years I spent as a coach at amateur and youth levels, I am glad that I experienced life as an official because I learned so much more from my time in the job.

Most of the abusive comments I heard as a referee were easy to ignore although sometimes, just sometimes, they could be quite hurtful. I also occasionally heard laugh out loud comments that I acknowledged and took in good part. I have never had a problem laughing at myself and I did not mind others having a dig at me in the absence of malice. By the way, I am fully aware of the fact that most of the people who gather around pitches to cheer on their amateur or youth club teams do not make many mistakes, particularly concerning football. Let me make a confession. In my playing days and in the 10 years I spent at Valspar Football Club as a parent, coach, manager, committee member and chairman, I believed that I had a good understanding of the laws of the game and I was quick to disagree with referee decisions before, during and after matches. I discovered how wrong

I was during my referee training and after passing the exam that authorised my participation in matches as an official. I have a hunch that most people who contribute a vocal opinion on the interpretation of the laws of the game from the side of any pitch could not tell you how many laws there are, far less what they are and what they mean. Nevertheless, many feel that it is their duty to ridicule one of the very few people who make it their business to know the laws inside out.

My first appointment as a referee was on 17 February 2007 in Dalrymple. The 13s match ended in an 11-0 win for Crosshouse and the match passed without incident. 'This refereeing lark is easy,' I thought to myself. On the very same day, Ayr United travelled to Greenock and they were turned over 4-2. Now that I had my own matches to go to, I could just about forgive myself for deserting my team in their hour of need. It took a while but I eventually got the hang of seeing the game from a variety of positions on the field, instead of standing in one position at the touchline. Remembering how I appealed decisions constantly from the side when I was coaching Valspar, I learned quickly to take the comments from the side of the park with a pinch of salt. I could relate to the situation of the coaches who wanted the best for their teams but I had a completely new perspective now. Most of the people I had to speak to during a match were guilty of letting their emotions take over and in the heat of the moment it was understandable. After only a few matches, I was given my first big test. It may only have been a 12s match but the teams contesting the match were Valspar and Ayr Boswell. Comments before kick-off from the Ayr Boswell support included references to my allegiance to Valspar, while the Valspar contingent were suggesting that I would probably favour Boswell to prove conclusively that I had cut ties with my former club. Both parties made sure that I was able to hear their predictions and it seemed like I would be portrayed as the villain for any of the teams losing. Now that's the kind of pressure that a referee is put under before a match and we are talking about a non-competitive match between 12-year-olds. As you may imagine, the only problems I had in the match came from the sidelines. The players were absolutely fine and there was no need for a single caution. It was apparent, from the early stages of the second period, that Ayr Boswell were in control of the match and at 2-1 up in the dying moments of the game, they put the result beyond doubt with a third goal. When I blew the final whistle I expected handshakes all round but instead I was confronted by an irate Valspar coach. He sprinted over to me and immediately started ranting about the 'fact' that I had blown the whistle three minutes early. '…we could've got back into this game,' he shouted in a voice that had become a high pitched squeal. 'I timed the second half on this watch and you can see there's another three minutes to go,' he continued. I felt it necessary to resort to sarcasm. 'I timed it too and as you can see…' I pointed to my own watch, '…the match is over. I can maybe help you though…there's a wee shop in Queen's Court, up the Sandgate…they could have a look at that watch for you. They do all sorts of repairs.' As I turned away he muttered, 'Fuckin' funny man.' If I had tried that approach in different circumstances, with different people, I could well have ended up in hospital but it's all about assessing the situation and acting accordingly.

In late February 2009, I accepted two match appointments over a weekend and sandwiched in between the two matches was Ayr United's home match against Brechin City as well as a Saturday night trip to the cinema with my wife. Now that was my idea of an enjoyable weekend. It was a very cold Saturday morning at King George V as I arrived to take control of a 14s match between Ayr Thistle and Valspar. It was so cold that I decided to wear my recently purchased long john's and as I stepped onto pitch four, I was greeted by a well built gentleman, breathing into his cupped hands before giving them a good rub, creating the friction that would provide him with what little heat he could muster. 'Oh, lovely new tights ref, that'll protect these lily white thighs underneath. You'll be nice and toasty in these and they're sexy ones into the bargain.' That's the kind of harmless banter I can accept any day of the week. The joke was on me and I acknowledged the humour while everyone around had a good laugh at my expense.

In a nice relaxed atmosphere, both teams put everything into a well-contested match with Valspar eventually running out 2-0 winners. After shaking hands with the players and coaches at the end of the match, I made my way off the park and there was the same chap with the quick wit, ready with the next instalment of his comedy routine. He must have heard the coaches calling me by name during the match and he personalised his approach this time. 'Good game Gerry! I'll definitely need to get myself a pair of these tights. Where did you buy them, La Senza?' I couldn't help but laugh, as I jokingly reprimanded him for disrespecting me. It was a good start to the weekend.

A short drive home from Heathfield, a bath, a bite to eat and Marilyn joined me, on a rare Saturday off for her, to take in the match at Somerset Park between Ayr and Brechin. The second instalment of my fun filled two days was another source of great satisfaction. Despite losing two early goals to Brechin, Ayr played some nice stuff as they stormed back with four of their own, including a double from Mark Roberts, to win the match 4-2. It was a very enjoyable afternoon's football for us and I hailed Marilyn as our new lucky charm. My incident-free match in the morning, and a win for the 'Honest Men' in the afternoon, set us up for a nice relaxed evening out at the cinema in Kilmarnock. We had heard good reports about *Slumdog Millionaire* and it turned out to be a good choice of film. Part of the entertainment, before the movie got underway, was both coincidental and hilarious. As we made our way through the already darkened auditorium, Marilyn took my arm as we climbed the stairs. We shuffled into a row of seats and settled down as the adverts beamed across the screen. Suddenly, a man sitting directly in front of us, turned towards us and spoke up quite loudly, 'Have you still got your La Senza tights on Gerry?' I squinted to get a better look at the man and discovered that it was the guy from the side of the pitch at the morning match I had refereed. What were the chances of us both ending up in the same place, on the same night. On the drive from Ayr to Kilmarnock, I had been telling Marilyn about my quick-witted tormentor and she had found it very amusing. Now, she was being treated to an encore, as if to verify the authenticity of my story. The man must have told his wife about the incident as it was clear from her response to the interaction that she understood exactly what it was all about. With the four of us in stitches laughing, the other people around us must have been wondering what it was all about.

On the afternoon of the next day, Sunday 22 February 2009, I took to the park at Dalrymple to handle the local club's age 17s match against Stevenston Thistle. My only concern ahead of kick-off time was related to a group of youngsters sitting at the side of the pitch. They were drinking from cans of beer and they had a sizeable 'carry out' sitting at their feet. The age group for the match suggested that it would be a blood and guts, testosterone-filled contest between two teams determined to prove that they were stronger, more skilled and more committed than their opponents. Unfortunately, a smashing game of football between two evenly-matched teams eventually descended into scenes more akin to a saloon brawl from a wild west movie. After 85 minutes, the home team were leading 4-3 and their fancied opponents were none too pleased about the way it was going. Although the game had been contested in a very sporting manner, I had issued only two yellow cards in the time we had played. One moment of madness ignited a spark that ruined the game as a spectacle as mayhem ensued. As a Dalrymple player carried the ball towards the Stevenston goal, he contemplated a shot from about 25 yards out. His opponent lunged into a tackle and caught the Dalrymple player's thigh with his studs. It was a horrendous tackle. I blew my whistle, waved on the Dalrymple first-aider and beckoned the Stevenston player towards me. He knew what the punishment was going to be and when I raised the red card he muttered, 'Fair enough ref'. As the player walked towards the away team's touchline, I noticed a Stevenston player sprinting over to one of his opponents. He barged the player and challenged him to a fight but as soon as I sounded my whistle he had second thoughts and backed off. I took him aside and, after taking his name, I showed him a red card and pointed to the pavilion. He accepted the decision and followed his teammate to the touchline.

When players are ordered from the field of play they must always go to the dressing room and cannot stay at the side of the park, so I jogged over to where they were standing and informed the Stevenston coach that both players would need to go to the pavilion. As I spoke to them, one of the adults standing nearby suddenly started shouting incoherently as he pointed to something behind me. I turned to see every player on the field engaged in hand-to-hand combat. Punches and kicks were being exchanged between both sets of players and at that moment I knew the game was over. All I could do was take up a position in the middle of the park and take notes as the battle continued. As if things were not bad enough, the young drinkers at the side of the pitch decided to join in and as they raced onto the park to add to the affray, my eye caught a tall guy, probably in his late teens. He strode up behind a Stevenston player and caught the boy flush on his face with a right hook. The boy fell to the ground and lay there for some time with the fights carrying on all around him. I wrote a few notes in my book, describing the cowardly assailant who had attacked the player.

Several people had called the police but it would be another 15 minutes before they arrived. Meanwhile, the man I had identified as the head coach of Stevenston Thistle walked over to my observation point on the pitch and proceeded to give me a piece of his mind. 'This whole thing is out of control and aw you can dae is staun there with yer wee notebook…' I was not sure what he expected of me but he seemed to be implying that I should be attempting to break up the fights. The gentleman who was criticising me was a giant of a man, weighing around 20 stone. He continued, '…if you're no' gonnae dae somethin', I will'. He stormed off as I cast my eye over the crowd in a vain bid to see where the thug had gone after assaulting the Stevenston player. The next thing I knew, some of the Dalrymple players were claiming that the giant coach threatened them with a hammer he had in the boot of his car. The situation was deteriorating and, to be honest, I hadn't a clue what I should do next.

To my great relief, three police cars, blue lights flashing and sirens screaming, arrived almost together and they were then followed by two large white police vans. The sight of a dozen police officers racing towards the scene was enough to bring an abrupt halt to the hostilities. When the dust settled, I officially abandoned the match and the police spent half an hour taking statements from partisan witnesses, before taking no action. To be fair, there was nothing much they could do. I spoke to the police about the nasty assault I had witnessed but the young thug was nowhere to be seen and they were not terribly interested in pursuing the assailant as nobody had suffered any long-lasting injury. It was incidents such as this that made me question my desire to continue refereeing but the vast majority of the time that I was involved in matches was pleasurable, to the extent that it at least outweighed the occasional flashpoints that blunted my enthusiasm.

A New Leader

When Brian Reid took over the helm at Ayr United back in October 2007 it gave me and all the other Ayr supporters something to hope for. A new young manager who could perhaps turn around our fortunes and maybe even take us out of the Second Division and back to mediocrity in Division One. His first full season in charge held some promise as Ayr battled their way to the First Division Play-offs. Brechin did not present too big a problem in the two-legged semi-final, so it was down to home and away matches against Airdrie with the reward of First Division status to the winners. Airdrie had endured a horrific season but they would be spared relegation from the First Division if they could beat Ayr United, the best of the Second Division play-off hopefuls.

With the first leg at Somerset, it was important for Ayr to establish a lead in the tie but, as any Ayr supporter will testify, it is seldom as straightforward as that with our team. By half-time we were two goals down and it looked like another long season of ignominy in the Second Division would be our fate. The usual small group of bigmouths in the Somerset Road end were blasting

Brian Reid for what was admittedly a very poor first half performance from the team. These people seem to relish the thought of the team losing, so you can imagine their disappointment when Ayr came out in the second half with all guns blazing. A double from 'Marko' Roberts, the first after only three minutes of the second half, saw Ayr level the match and, although it was not the ideal result, we could prepare for the journey to the Shyberry Excelsior (or whatever they are calling it this weather) with a realistic hope of success. It seemed to be a regular feature of the season, Ayr would give their opponents a couple of goals of a start before they started playing in earnest. Now that it was down to the final match of the season, the team had to get it right.

Once again we readied ourselves for another great day out, bedecked in black and white, we joined another 2,000 Ayr fans in the journey to Airdrie in the hope that our team could pull off the result that would bring us promotion. The magnificent Ayr support played their part on the day, with a loud and vociferous backing of the team and a good strike from Ryan Stevenson was enough to take us back into division one. It was not the most inspiring game of football but there was a moment in the match that made the hairs on the back of my neck stand up. It was as if I had been whisked back to the 1970s when Johnny Doyle had the ball at his feet and he was running at the opposition full-back. The Somerset Road end of the ground would erupt, as the crowd got right behind the team. The very thought of those days brings a tear to my eyes. With five minutes left in the First Division Play-off Final in 2009, Ayr were in possession of the ball in their own half of the field. Suddenly, for no apparent reason, the noise in the stand grew to a crescendo. The entire Ayr support was willing the team across the finish line. That recent memory is now indelibly marked on my mind, available at any time, so that I can bask in that relative glory I keep banging on about. When 'Stevo' opened the scoring, a text was soon winging its way to Ben. Marilyn had promised to keep him up to date with how things were going and he texted straight back to say that he wished he was with us in Airdrie. He had remained faithful to his team on the day and was sitting in Parkhead watching Celtic grind out a 0-0 draw against Hearts. It served as a lesson to our estranged offspring that there's no place like home, or in this case, Airdrie. It just goes to show that supporting my wee team can sometimes be an altogether more attractive proposition than following a supposed giant of world football.

As is customary on such an occasion, the final whistle heralded the start of joyous celebrations. The Airdrie fans trooped off home in disgust as the Ayr fans invaded the pitch to celebrate. When the police finally restored order, the Ayr team re-emerged from the pavilion to thank the supporters. The full array of songs and chants rang out and the players joined in, draped in Ayr scarves and wearing black and white jester hats. Brian Reid brought his wife and children onto the pitch-side to receive the acclaim of the Ayr faithful and he deservedly took a bow for his excellent efforts in putting together the promotion winning squad. One particularly funny moment was when Dean Keenan swapped his football boots for a supporter's Doc Martens and as the singing reached fever pitch, 'Deano' danced along to 'Ayr, Ayr, Super Ayr' and 'We are, going up, say, we are going up'

Our celebrations were adjourned as we returned to Ayr before meeting up at the house of our friends in Masonhill to party on into the evening. Stevie and Karlene laid on the food and when we all arrived with our carry-outs, we danced, sang and generally enjoyed our moment of relative glory. This is what being an Ayr United supporter is all about. There would be time for the dissenters to get back on Brian Reid's back but for the time being we were all one big happy family. For our victory party we had a rule, if anyone walked up the steps to the higher 'plateau' of the garden, they were obliged to sing, 'We are going up, say, we are going up,' as they negotiated the steps. Of course mingled among our songs there was a spattering of derogatory songs about our fierce rivals Kilmarnock. 'Monkey's Heid', 'Raking through buckets', 'Paper Hankies' etc, etc. Ayr United were back in the First Division and the next big target would be the team's survival in the higher league.

As the new season developed, I missed a lot of games because of my commitment to refereeing but every time I turned up at Somerset Park I felt that I was being punished for my absence. A depressing October of injury for me, coincided with an even more depressing run of defeats for Ayr. Defeats at Firhill and Airdrie sandwiched a 5-1 home massacre at the hands of Inverness Caledonian Thistle. Of course, I had no such injury problems during the 'Honest Men's' mini-revival in the early part of 2010, so the season was just one big misery for me. On the whole, Ayr United were found wanting. They just could not cut it in the First Division and they were sent spinning back into Division Two to think again. The celebrations at Airdrie the previous season were consigned to history and it was back to the drawing board for Brian Reid and the 'Honest Men'.

Tales of the Touchline

My season officiating in youth football, meanwhile, was fairly uneventful. In fact, in the 35 games I refereed, I issued only six red cards and 34 yellow cards. My matches spanned all age groups from 13 to 19 and taking everything into consideration, the players were relatively well behaved. The touchlines were a slightly different matter however.

Referees, on a regular basis, can expect to receive calls at short notice from harassed match secretaries trying to replace officials who have called off because of injury or illness. In one of my injury-free periods, I answered one such call of distress from Tom Johnston of the West of Scotland Youth Football League. He had a late call-off on a Saturday night and needed a ref to cover a 17s match the following day at Hurlford, where the home team had a league match against Caledonian from Prestwick. Tom filled me in on the bad feeling that had developed between the two teams over a long period and advised me to be on my guard. On arrival at the ground I was greeted by two Hurlford officials. They were very well mannered, articulate gentlemen who made me feel welcome and they thanked me for standing in at short notice. The same two men did get around to warning me about their opponents and how they would stoop to all sorts of underhanded behaviour to secure a victory. I let these comments go in one ear and out the other as I was not prepared to let one side or the other influence my decision-making. When the away team arrived, the Caledonian coach said very little. He cast no aspersions on the other team and just got on with the job of preparing his team for what was a top of the table encounter. After completing my warm up, I walked onto the pitch from behind one of the goals, checked the nets and continued walking towards the far away goal to repeat the task. As I walked past the Hurlford team, who were passing several balls around, one of the balls fell at my feet. I was standing about 20-yards from the goal line and when I jokingly gestured to shoot, the goalkeeper shouted over to me, 'Come on then, give us a laugh ref'. He was positioned on the six-yard line and I couldn't resist the temptation to take him on. I measured my shot and lifted my effort high into the air, over his outstretched arms and into the back of the net. For some reason, the Hurlford players were astonished and I think the reason for the surprise is that they had a stereotypical perception of me. You know, referees know nothing about football. This one certainly could never have played football and being over 50 would not have the wherewithal to kick a ball with any effect. As I wore my smile proudly, I was treated to a burst of spontaneous applause from all the Hurlford players, including the beaten 'keeper. If anything, I had grown in their estimation of me but I detected a hint of ridicule mixed in with the flattering comments. Having spoken to the Caledonian team as I checked their boots, I was entirely at ease with the task of handling the match as both sets of players and coaches seemed reasonable people who were focused on enjoying the match.

I totally misjudged the situation and I was given a rude awakening straight after kick-off. A gold-shirted Caledonian player was in possession of the ball close to the touchline where the Hurlford coaches and substitutes were standing and as he ran towards his opponents' goal, the Hurlford number six, resplendent in his sky blue strips, came sliding in with a late tackle. As the victim writhed in pain on the floor, he was subjected to a variety of verbally abusive comments from the coaches and subs of the home team. His crime was to have been hacked down by his unscrupulous opponent and he was being vehemently chastised for allowing it to happen. Two minutes in and the first yellow card was produced, along with a word of warning to the abusers. The player recovered on his own and as his teammate gave him a short free kick to get his team back on the attack, the same player who moments ago was the victim was upended by the same player who committed the first offence. Two and a half minutes on the clock and the second yellow card was followed by a red. It was a no-brainer. As I sent the player off, the gentlemen coaches of Hurlford turned their attentions to me and my apparent ineptitude. Apparently I had been conned by the diving Caledonian player, who was subsequently helped from the field of play and substituted.

Despite several warnings, the smart comments of the Hurlford contingent at the sidelines continued. To be honest, some of it was really quite funny. 'Where's the real referee?…in the boot of your car?' 'Did you get that referee's outfit on E-Bay?' I'm perfectly alright with that type of ridicule. Unfortunately, the conduct on the touchline deteriorated as the match slipped away from the home side. The truth is that their opponents were outplaying them and when Caledonian scored the opening goal, the behaviour of the Hurlford officials and players deteriorated further. Two yellow cards in quick succession for the impetuous Hurlford goalkeeper, early in the second half, left them with nine players and a mountain to climb and when the away team made it 2-0 it was apparent that my biggest task would be to prevent the match from spiralling out of control. Of course, if the game turns nasty it will be the referee to blame. It seems that in situations like this, despite the outrageous antics of players, coaches and spectators, attention turns to the referee to justify the moronic behaviour of these people. I am particularly fond of the comment, 'He's lost it,' meaning that I've lost control of the match. In this match the home side had, 'lost it'. Their players were out of control and two of them also lost their places on the field of play.

Fortunately, on this occasion the nine remaining Hurlford players accepted their defeat and played out the match with no further deterioration of their on-field discipline. In retrospect, I should have sent both Hurlford officials to the dressing room long before the end of the match but I believed that they wouldn't have gone without causing major problems and it could have ended with an abandonment of the match. With a few minutes to go, the Caledonian official who took on the role of linesman for the match, raised his flag to signal that the ball had run out of play. I was positioned about 20 yards infield from the touchline and as I could not see the line clearly,

I blew my whistle to acknowledge that the ball had gone out of play. The Hurlford coaches decided there and then that the ball had not gone out of play and that the linesman was cheating to give his side an advantage. It was impossible for them to see that far but they began shouting insults and threats at their counterparts on the opposite touchline. One comment that went too far was, 'I'm going to come over there and stick that flag right up your fuckin' arse, ya fuckin' bastard'. It was more than enough for me to take further action but I decided to complete the match before dealing with it. I blew the final whistle with the score still at 2-0 and as I walked off the park, players from both sides shook my hand. The Hurlford coaches made a beeline for me, to criticise my handling of the game and to verbalise their version of incidents that had taken place. I interrupted them to insist that they come to my changing room where I would speak to them. I then approached the Caledonian manager and asked him to come to my changing room to act as a witness. When everyone was assembled, I explained to the Hurlford officials that I would be submitting an incident report with details of the verbal abuse and threats directed at the Caledonian official. When both of the individuals tried to argue with me, I refused to respond and pointed out that they would receive a copy of my report and they would have an opportunity to respond at the disciplinary meeting convened by the West of Scotland League. What happened next made me glad that I followed protocol by ensuring that the Caledonian manager was present as a witness. Both Hurlford officials flew into a rage and called me a variety of names, using every expletive that I could ever come up with. To say that I was alarmed was an understatement and but for the Caledonian manager intervening to calm the guys down, I may have been slapped around a bit for good measure. They eventually stormed out of the room and all I could hear was what sounded like kicking of doors and objects being thrown around the home dressing room.

The subsequent disciplinary meeting at Auchincruive College some weeks later saw a complete contrast in the behaviour of the two people involved. They were calm and controlled as they spoke eloquently in answer to the charges brought against them. When it came to my turn, I declared that my report was completely accurate and that I had nothing to add. When the Caledonian manager was questioned as a witness, he was as diplomatic as possible but agreed with everything I had reported. The conduct of the Hurlford officials in my changing room after the match made it so much worse for themselves. If they had accepted that they would be disciplined for their touchline behaviour, they would undoubtedly have received discipline but their antics after the match became the biggest issue in the eyes of the disciplinary committee. One of the most annoying things for referees in these situations is that we are never informed of the disciplinary action taken. I am not sure of the reasons for this but invariably these individuals eventually return to the touchline and, in my experience, they rarely change their ways.

Ahead of the 2010-11 season, I was contacted by the match secretary of the Ayrshire Amateur League to ask if I would consider stepping up from youth football and, after gaining permission from the Association Manager of Ayrshire Referees, I decided to give it a go. Although I had enjoyed working in youth games, I relished the rough and tumble, blood and guts world of amateur football. The first big difference I noticed between the two grades was the noise on the park. In youth football, all the noise came from the touchlines. The players in amateur football are a noisy bunch and are constantly shouting at one another. Add to that the outrageous coaches and spectators and you have bedlam most of the time. It took me a few games to get used to the increased volume but once I did I found my job more enjoyable than before.

Part of the attraction of refereeing for me was the enjoyment to be derived from the interaction with the players on the park, the coaches and managers on the touchline and the spectators who attend the matches. In any run of the mill matches at youth and amateur level, the crowd rarely gets above 50 people but you can be sure that in among that number there will be a few people who will add positively to the occasion with witty remarks and banter. Having already given details of nasty incidents that I have witnessed during my time in football, this may seem a little contradictory. However, it is not all bad. I need to mention some of the lighter moments, the quick quips, the banter, the put downs and some of the funny things that happen at a public park near you.

I had been refereeing amateur games for only a few weeks when I was assigned to a Second Division league match in Ayr between Wallacetoun AFC and Dalry Amateurs. It was a Wednesday evening match played at Voluntary Park in Whitletts. The home ground of Junior League side Whitletts Victoria doubled up as a greyhound track. The greyhound track had been situated there since the move from Limekiln Road, over at the

Tam's Brig area of the town, over 30 years before. Wallacetoun were taking advantage of the availability of the park in midweek to fulfil their league fixture against their North Ayrshire opposition.

This was one of these games that make refereeing a pleasure. I arrived at the ground 40 minutes before kick-off time and was greeted by the Wallacetoun officials who were friendly and courteous. The Dalry team arrived in buoyant mood, full of good humour and up for the match and we got underway in perfect conditions for a match, a warm and sunny August evening.

With the home team leading by a goal to nil and the game becoming a bit one sided, the visitors surprised us all. In a break from defence they managed to get a good cross into the opposition box and just as their tall number nine went up to head the ball, he was nudged off the ball. I pointed to the penalty mark and ran to take up a position on the goal line. I cautioned the offender before the penalty was converted to bring the scores level, much to the chagrin of the home team and their 20 or so supporters on the touchline.

A fired-up Wallacetoun then took back control of the game and Dalry's defence was shaking as the home team threatened to overwhelm them. The Dalry coach, who was running the line for his team, was shouting instructions to his players and becoming increasingly frustrated at their antics in clearing the ball with various parts of the human anatomy. After the latest calamity, which almost resulted in an own goal, he was incandescent with rage. 'What are you doing back there?...' he shouted, '...it's like a pantomime'. Now, no matter if I'm in the middle of a match refereeing, at home with my family or in a classroom with students, I can never resist the temptation to blurt out what I believe is a funny response to a comment such as this one. My hysterically humorous riposte was, 'Oh n-o-o-o-o it isn't'. There are a lot of football coaches out there who do not take kindly to smart mouth comments like that, particularly from a referee. I'm glad to say that this guy took it in the spirit it was intended and we had a good laugh about it.

When it comes to smart comments, I would freely admit that I am not in the same league as some of the people who surround the touchlines of youth and amateur football and one such comment reduced everyone in the ground to hysterical laughter. Wallacetoun had finished the game as a contest with two quick goals inside a minute and they were spreading the ball across the park as the Dalry team tired. A terrific diagonal pass from the home team's number six sent the ball out to the right flank and although the Wallacetoun winger was a bit of a speed merchant, there was no way he could have reached the pass as it was too heavy. The ball ran out of play 10 yards in front of the intended target. It was then that the booming voice of a gentleman from the crowd delivered his timely one liner. 'I ken we're at a dog track but he's no' a fuckin' greyhound'. It was a small nugget of comedy gold from the terrace.

Wallacetoun added another goal before the end of the game and although the 4-1 scoreline was probably deserved, the away team had contributed greatly to a well-contested match. Dalry were magnanimous in defeat and it was handshakes all round. Now, that was a good way to pass an evening. I suppose it took matches like that to outweigh the negative aspects of the game and this kept me enthusiastic about my pastime.

A Premature End

During my stint as a referee I became accustomed to the reality that I would need to tolerate outrageous conduct, verbal abuse and mickey taking. I always felt that I could control these situations and that it would not stop me refereeing for years to come. I was wrong.

April 2011 arrived and a major incident was just around the corner and unfortunately it led to my resignation as a referee. I felt that I was left with no alternative after an evening of intimidation, threats and the outrageous conduct of players and spectators in an amateur league match I handled. I travelled to Girvan to referee the Vale of Girvan versus Doon Amateurs match at Victory Park in the town. It was a warm evening, perfect for football and I was fit and raring to go. The home team had been enjoying a successful season and a comfortable win against the Third Division bottom dogs was on the cards. The fine weather brought out a much larger than expected crowd that I estimated at 200. I wasn't surprised to see a group of testosterone-filled guys making a dent in the sizeable drinks carry-out they brought along for their evening's entertainment. They were a mix of teenagers and a few men in their 20s and 30s. I did notice a few scary looking characters amongst them and I was a little concerned about the fact that they had set up their camp just behind the goal nearest the pavilion. The Doon goalkeeper was at the opposite end of the pitch in the first half so he would not be harangued for the first 45 minutes. I had not come across the Doon team in my travels but I had refereed Vale of Girvan matches three times. I was well aware of what to expect from their players and officials. Like a lot of teams, their players questioned every decision and I usually had a running conversation with them as I tried to keep the game flowing. Their team manager was a large, loud and aggressive man who was prone to frequent temper tantrums when things were going badly for his team. In every Vale of Girvan match I was appointed to, his emotions ran away with him and although he spent the 90 minutes of every match loudly criticising my decisions, he always shook my hand at the final whistle and apologised for his behaviour. He had a large audience on this particular night and he seemed to enjoy the limelight.

The early part of the match saw most of the play taking place in and around the Doon penalty area. Nevertheless, 15 minutes passed with no breakthrough for the home side. The mood of the crowd was still relaxed, despite the fact that the Dalmellington team were gradually working their way into the game and in one fast break the Girvan goalkeeper had to be off his line quickly to intercept a long ball to the lone Doon striker. Every time the away side played the ball to their number 11 they looked threatening. He was a small, speedy, 'tanner ba' player who was prepared to take players on. With 10 minutes left of the first half Doon upset the odds by taking the lead. The wee winger who had been causing more and more problems for the home side went on a solo run that ended with a beautifully placed shot wide of the diving 'keeper to make it 1-0. The same player then brought out the best in Vale of Girvan's goalkeeper, who dived full length to touch the ball onto a post to prevent Doon from doubling their lead. The Vale manager was getting quite heated and spurred his team on with constructive shouts such as, 'Get a fuckin' grip' and, 'Come oan tae fuck you lot'.

The first moment of controversy came when a Vale striker burst into the box only to take a heavy touch. This gave the Doon 'keeper an opportunity to dive at the feet of the attacker and as he collected the ball, the Girvan player tried a swallow dive over the prone body of the goalkeeper. The screams for a penalty from the home touchline were quite hysterical and there was not the remotest chance of me awarding it. The Vale of Girvan manager, as I could have expected, then turned his attention to my performance and from that moment to the very end of the match he never let up. As I sounded the half-time whistle, I saw the break as an opportunity to let things calm down a bit and although the Vale manager remonstrated with me as we left the field, he realised his protests would not help him. I did explain to him that I would not allow him to continue shouting abusive remarks at me from the touchline in the second half but his response was, 'nae fuckin' wunner,' which I translated as 'no wonder'.

As I walked towards the pavilion the drunks behind the goal gave me a roasting. You know the kind of thing, questioning my parenthood etc. There was nothing very inventive about it and it went in one ear and out the other. The only contentious moment of the first half had been the validity of the penalty claim from the home side. They had piled the pressure on me with their big Jessie screams in the hope that I would cave in. It never worked. There had been one booking for each side in the first period and little else of significance took place. The Vale player that I cautioned was, coincidentally, a student of mine. The fact that he called me by my Christian name, making it obvious to everyone that he knew me, made me determined to show my objectivity. So the fact never saved him from his booking for deliberately tripping his opponent.

The second half followed the same pattern as the first. Vale pressing for an equaliser and Doon looking dangerous on the break. I was particularly pleased with my fitness levels as the game progressed. I was sprinting into position well and I was right on top of the play to give strong decisions and take the heat out of any potentially explosive confrontations. In the same way as I can recognise when my performance is poor, I was delighted with the way I was handling this match. The big, loud Girvan manager was a bit of a nuisance, with his constant criticism of my decisions, but no more than that. His team were still behind with 20 minutes to go, against a team that on paper should have offered little resistance, so he needed someone to blame.

Things were about to get a whole lot worse for his team however. The scorer of the first goal had not been contained and as he made another darting run into the penalty area, the Vale goalkeeper rushed from his line to dive at his feet. A little sidestep took the Doon man clear and as he attempted to slide the ball into the empty net, the Vale right back could only manage to scythe down the striker before he could complete his task. I pointed to the penalty mark as I blew on my whistle. The player who committed the offence never complained about the penalty award and when I subsequently showed the offender a red card for denying a clear goal-scoring opportunity, there was a general acceptance from all the players that it was the only logical conclusion. He walked forlornly to the pavilion as the victim recovered to slot the ball home to make it 2-0.

The now apoplectic, red-faced Girvan manager had a slightly different perspective. The reason his team were losing by two goals was solely down to my inept performance, apparently. 'You should never be allowed to referee another game.' 'You're a silly old bastard that should have retired 20 years ago.' There was plenty more where that came from and when his substitutes and some of the crowd on the touchline joined in with the abuse, I decided to have a quiet word with him. I reminded him of his responsibility to control himself and the others on his touchline but he was beyond reasoning and wanted only to argue with me about the perfectly straightforward decisions being made. Some of my colleagues, and certainly my supervisors, would argue that I should have sent him to the pavilion at that point. To be honest, I can fully understand those who would criticise me for being a soft touch who needs to be firmer and who should take sanctions against people like this man. However, I can relate to people who are passionate and get carried away at football matches. Another reason for letting him remain at the side was that the touchline could have become even more chaotic and I would not have had a channel to communicate. I suppose that I was hoping that my words of caution would perhaps calm him down and that he would deal with the more outrageous behaviour as it escalated. The drunks behind the goal were becoming more vociferous in their condemnation of the under-fire match official and for the first time in my career as a referee I was treated to a chorus of 'The referee's a wanker'. It was a proud moment for me. I had finally reached the same level of regard afforded referees at the very top level. I could not help but be thankful that I was having a good game.

It is amazing what a goal can do to change the atmosphere at a football match. With 10 minutes to go, the Vale of Girvan team interrupted the hostilities to fashion together a flowing move that ended with a well-taken strike to reduce the deficit. I went from Public Enemy Number One to the Invisible Man as everyone in Victory Park ignored me to concentrate on the football. The Vale manager stopped criticising me and instead urged his team on in a total transformation from his earlier demeanour. He even encouraged and praised his players. I was delighted to be out of the limelight. When the equaliser arrived right on the 90-minute mark, the Gunfight at the OK Corral became the Sound of Music. If the Vale of Girvan manager had burst into a rendition of *My Favourite Things* it would not have been out of place. I had decided to add six minutes at 2-2 because of stoppages for injury, one being a dislocated shoulder for a Doon player. The away team had gone from two goals up to hanging on for a draw and the Girvan team sensed that the win was within their grasp. The away team survived wave after wave of attacks and with time running out Girvan won a corner at the pavilion end of the pitch. I took up my position level with the six-yard line at the back post as Vale piled their players into the box to try and force a winner before the end. As the high ball floated into the box, the Girvan number five pushed the back of his opponent with both hands before heading the ball downwards towards the goal. As the ball fell at the feet of a Vale player, I sounded my whistle to signal a free-kick to the team defending but the Girvan player followed through, blasting the ball into the net. I blew my whistle again and gestured to the spot where the offence occurred as I pointed away from the goal. I was immediately engulfed by Vale of Girvan players who were suddenly back in wild west mode. Every referee has to deal with difficult decisions and with angry players who do not agree with these decisions. If you cannot handle these confrontational incidents, you're maybe not cut out for the job.

However, what I was subjected to on that evening went beyond protests and dissent. The Girvan player, a 6ft 5in 'tank' of a man in his 30s, who committed the offence, sprinted towards me. He had clearly lost his temper. He and I both knew that he had clearly pushed the Doon player but he never let that influence his decision. He greeted me with the words, 'That's fuckin' it. I've had enough of you, ya useless fuckwit,' as he drew his fist back to hit me. I knew there was no way I could avoid the inevitable knockout punch but as I prepared for the impact, a team mate of my assailant saw what was about to happen and dragged the big man back. As he cursed and swore at me, my saviour calmed him down and convinced him that accepting a yellow card would be better than missing an upcoming Cup Final. He eventually agreed and as I took him aside he only spoke to give me his name and number. Perhaps I should have been overwhelmed by the intimidation that I suffered. I was certainly badly shaken by the experience but being the type of person that I am, I felt it necessary to be true to myself, whatever the consequences. 'I'm sending you off for using offensive, insulting or abusive language,' I said to him as I raised the red card. He swung at the card, attempting to knock it out of my hand but he missed. He then pulled off his jersey as he stormed off the pitch. As he reached the door of the pavilion, his manager reverted back to type, giving me dog's abuse for sending off his player. I can only assume that he thought it was reasonable for the big fellow to attempt an assault on me and to curse and swear and be generally out of control with impunity. With only three minutes left, I let him continue his rant. As if things were not bad enough, my errant student, the one who was booked in the first half, jumped up with his opponent and inextricably punched the ball to knock it away from the Doon player. After awarding the free kick to Doon, I called him over and pulled out my notebook. 'No, Gerry…' he shouted loudly '…ye cannae book me, I've got a Cup Final coming up. Please, ye cannae book me'. I had no choice but to produce a second yellow card, followed by a red and once again there were howls of derision. The Vale of Girvan manager summed up the mood with another of his almost incoherent rants, 'You are an absolute fucking disgrace of a referee'.

A retired refereeing colleague of mine once gave me some tongue-in-cheek advice that was both humorous and thought provoking. He said something like this: 'If you are refereeing a match…and you find that you are not capable of controlling 22 players in a simple game of football…get rid of a couple.'

On this particular evening I had sent off three players but it never made it any easier. It was a release to blow the final whistle with the match ending in a draw. My relief was short-lived however. As I shook hands with the Doon manager, he decided to have his say. 'Poor performance ref, you gave them everything. They got a draw thanks to you,' he said as he walked off shaking his head. No sooner had I let go of his hand than the Vale of Girvan manager was at my side telling me how I had deliberately favoured Doon and cost his team the match. So, I apparently cost both teams the match. As we walked towards the changing rooms, the Vale manager fired questions at me before answering the questions himself. We were joined by four or five Vale players who joined in with the general abuse as we walked off the pitch and unknown to me, there was yet another ordeal just ahead. As I negotiated my way between the pitch and the pavilion, I was confronted by a posse from the group of drinkers behind the goal. A man in his mid-30s, with a shaved head and the body of a weightlifter, dressed in a tight fitting white tee-shirt and covered in tattoos blocked my path. As I tried to body-swerve the guy he stood in my way and fired off a question, 'How did ye no' gie that goal ya fuckin' clown?' The wit and repartee that I pride myself in would have been out of place in this situation but I desperately wanted to reply with, 'I think you'll find that it should be why did I not allow the goal'. I'm glad to report that I refrained from answering. No sooner had that thought disappeared when one of his mates reached over him to grab my top and drag me towards him. If it had not been for the intervention of several Vale of Girvan players, I believe that these mindless morons would have attacked me. The Vale players surrounded me and shepherded me into the relative safety of the changing rooms.

The Vale of Girvan captain accompanied his manager as they entered my dressing room to discuss the match. I gave clear explanations of my decisions and pointed out that along with the usual disciplinary reports from the match, I would be submitting an incident report with details of the manager's conduct and the intimidation and threats I was subjected to by spectators. The manager by this time was perfectly calm and reasonable. I did not fancy stepping back outside the pavilion into a baying crowd of drunks and I expressed my fears about leaving. 'I personally guarantee that you will get back to your car safely,' said the manager and he was as good as his word. He walked me out to my car and unbelievably, his last words to me before I left were, 'I'm sorry for all the trouble. You know me. I get caught up in the game. You never did anything wrong. We were rubbish and that's why we never won the game'. He was the one person who could have prevented all the trouble and here he was apologising when it was too late. Criticising referees is easy, even if they are blameless. I have admitted to having off days but on this particular evening I had an excellent match. It made no difference. Some people just do not know how to behave and the fact that it would not be changing in the foreseeable future made up my mind that it was time to call it a day.

I spent the next couple of weeks mulling over things and after a meeting with the Ayrshire Referees Association Manager, Dougie Smith, I took his advice and accepted an appointment of a youth match to try and get back into action and get my confidence back. I enjoyed an incident-free match but after weighing things up I decided to hang up my whistle. Dougie's advice was well intended and although I did not want to let the morons win, in truth, I was well beaten. I was offered the chance to take on a supervisory role with the association but instead I decided that I had contributed enough of my time to football in a variety of roles. My wife and kids wanted me to give up refereeing, purely from a safety angle, but the final decision was mine. I had envisaged years of refereeing ahead of me but after this experience I decided it was not worth all the hassle. Hence, my career as a referee reached a premature end. Instead of spending my Saturday afternoons being put under pressure to make decisions that suited biased, win-at-all-costs people, I would find another way to spend my Saturdays, doing something that I would enjoy. From the array of alternatives open to me, there was only going to be one winner.

The First Division Beckons... Again

I would go back to Somerset Park on a regular basis, for what was left of the 2010-11 season, and then I would buy my season ticket for 2011-12. There was no doubt the 'Honest Men' would be back in Division One by then. Despite the fact that Livingston were pulling away at the top of the Second Division, Ayr were well positioned to secure a play-off place and although our last foray into the higher league ended in tears, my bravado told me that Brian Reid, with more experience behind him, would consolidate our First Division status this time around. There was a small matter of winning the play-off semi-final and then the Final but when Cowdenbeath, Forfar and Brechin earned their places alongside Ayr, who eventually finished the Second Division campaign as runners-up, 23 points behind champions Livingston, I was fairly optimistic about the outcome. I never made it up to Angus for the first leg of the semi-final but apparently Forfar never offered any real resistance. The 4-1 scoreline in favour of Ayr made the second leg a formality and although Forfar earned a 3-3 draw at Somerset Park three days later, the 'Honest Men' were always going to progress to the Play-off

Final. We were in with a real chance of going straight back up after our relegation season and the two legged Final would be against Brechin City, who were too strong for Cowdenbeath in the other semi-final tie.

With the first leg of the Play-off Final at home, I attended the match with another 2,000 people, hoping that the right Ayr United team would turn up on the night. To be fair, they played very well and led with a first half strike from Michael Moffat. Ayr's new scoring sensation, signed from Girvan Juniors four months earlier, had already notched goals in both legs of the semi-final and as Ayr piled on the pressure, it looked like the tie would be over before our trip up north on the following Sunday. By the time the final whistle went however, ex Ayr United 'keeper Craig Nelson had denied the 'Honest Men' with several magnificent saves. 'Nelly' had kept his team's hopes alive and an equalising goal for Brechin with only a few minutes left gave the visitors an undeserved draw. We now had what amounted to a Cup Final to negotiate and the successful team would win promotion to the Irn Bru Scottish First Division. It was going to be another one of those exciting, nail-biting dramas; just like Airdrie two years previously and hopefully there would be a similar outcome.

On the morning of the match I was as excited as ever. Despite the fact that the Play-off Final should have been done and dusted in the first leg at Somerset Park, a part of me was glad that the game had ended in a 1-1 draw because it gave me, my family and friends another big day out to relish. 1,600 Ayr fans made the 284-mile round trip to the North East of the country to support the men in black and white and several factors contributed to the positivity that seemed to be surrounding the club at that time. Firstly, a new 'faction' was formed among the Ayr support and the group had been gathering momentum with every passing match. They called themselves the 'Somerset Ragazzi', a band of fervent youngsters who engage in non-stop singing and chanting in support of the team. In much the same way as we were maligned in the 70s for having hooligan tendencies, this group of youngsters seem to face prejudice wherever they go. Don't get me wrong; they are not angels. They are noisy, irreverent and tribal in their behaviour but on the whole, they are harmless and contribute positively to the atmosphere at games. It may be not have been members of the 'Ragazzi' to blame, but setting off flares and smoke bombs at matches just happened to coincide with the groups formation. I am all for this group of youngsters doing their thing, provided they conform to the legislation that is in place for everyone's safety at matches. Oh, and it would be good if they lost that infernal drum.

Confidence in the team's goalscoring prowess had developed dramatically with the introduction of Michael Moffat as Ayr's new striker in January 2011. He had been scoring regularly and although he would have been entitled to be proud of his successful transition from junior football to the senior game, he must have thought he was dreaming when he became an overnight cult hero, thanks mainly to a yet another new phenomenon about to emerge. The second positive factor came in the shape of someone who contributed greatly to Ayr United's 2010-11 season and he was one of us. He was a supporter, a fan, a follower... an 'Honest Man'. The phenomenon that is 'Somerset Boab' became an internet sensation when he posted a 'You Tube' video with his rendition of the Kings of Leon number *Your Sex On Fire*. He replaced the original lyrics with a tribute to Michael Moffat, entitled *The Moff Is On Fire* and it went down a bomb with the Ayr fans. So popular was 'Boab' that the club agreed to let him lead the Ayr supporters in song at the Play-off Final first leg at Somerset Park on 18 May. The whole crowd joined in with,'Yooouuuu, the Moff is on Fire'. It raised the roof in the Somerset Road end and the fans on the north terrace also contributed to something special as 'Boab'started off the sing-a-long from the family stand. I do not know why but occasions like this never fail to give me a lump in my throat. Sing on 'Boab'!

If these two additions to the support of Ayr United created a new, positive buzz about the place, the next additional factor complemented the influence of the 'Ragazzi' and 'Somerset Boab' with financial input to the club. Calvin Ayre brought with him shirt sponsorship for the team and although the reaction by some sections of the support was hysterical, the speculation that he may be lining up a takeover of the club gave the management, players and supporters yet another lift. These three elements combined to create excitement and anticipation of better times for the 'Honest Men' and I was one of many who welcomed the input of all three.

The Sunday morning of the Play-off Final at 10.30 was the agreed time of departure for our enthusiastic band of 'Honest Men and Bonnie Lassies'. We made the 142-mile journey to Brechin in our fleet of cars, ready for the big promotion push. For any away match, there are probably three of us who would travel but this game had appealed to many more of our glory-hunting family and friends. Marilyn, Ben, Karlene, Alan, Shona, David and

Rochelle joined me, Stevie and Andy. Three growing to 10 was probably the norm for the entire support, hence the reason that 1,600 travelled a long way for the match. If the weather on the way up the M9 was anything to go by, it was going to be a very uncomfortable day for the fans and a difficult task for the players on a surface that would undoubtedly be very heavy due to the excessive rainfall. As it turned out, I played my part in ensuring that the match conditions would be perfect for the occasion.

We arrived in Brechin just after 1pm and after parking at the local supermarket we made our way up the street to the pub to meet up with our party, Marilyn with a plastic carrier bag over her head to protect her hair against the heavy shower of rain that welcomed us to Angus. I then made my most telling move of the day by rushing into a filling station to purchase a cheap umbrella. No sooner had Marilyn opened the brolly above her head than the rain ceased. The sun came out and we were then treated to a perfect day for the occasion. A pint in Hudson's, followed by an excellent bag of chips up the road at the Ashvale Fish Restaurant, and we were ready for action. The rest of the day followed the same pattern as our previous play-off success at Airdrie. A large, vocal support, vastly outnumbering the home team fans, and tension from start to finish. Thanks to the extremely tolerant nature of the local police, there were no major incidents. For the umpteenth time, an idiot amongst us decided that it would be a good idea to let off a smoke bomb and in all the excitement, Ayr supporters indulged in two celebratory pitch invasions. Police in other areas of Scotland would do well to consider the strategy adopted by the team of police and stewards deployed at this match. They were non-confrontational, helpful and friendly. This is how it should be done. The growing problem, of flares and smoke bombs being set off at matches, needs to be addressed however. At best it causes discomfort for those in the vicinity and at worst there is a potential for injury to someone in the crowd.

At kick-off time, the sun was shining on Glebe Park and I was able to notch up a visit to a ground that I had never been to in my 40-odd years of travel with Ayr United. The distinctive privet hedge that runs along one side of the ground adds to the charm that the small stadium has. The huge roar at the first whistle from the 1,600 Ayr fans behind the goal and the 800 Brechin fans in the other areas of the ground should have spurred on the teams but in a dull first half there was little between the teams. I do not know if it was the weight of expectation that was causing the problem but

Ayr looked disjointed in the first half. It certainly was not pretty to watch and just before half-time, my stomach sank. Brechin opened the scoring. Well, to be more accurate, we opened the scoring for them. A high ball to the edge of the Ayr box landed on the three-penny bit head of Martyn Campbell and as his skewed header dropped to young Jonathan Tiffoney, he tried to guide it back to his goalkeeper only to see it evade Alan Martin and roll agonisingly into the back of the net.

Although Ayr played much better in the second half, I was fast running out of nails to bite before that pain in the neck Craig Nelson pulled off a double save that would have graced the World Cup Final, never mind the Scottish First Division Play-off Final. To be honest, I'd made up my mind that it wasn't going to be our day. The thought of playing another season in division two was quite depressing and it seemed that the calamitous error on the stroke of half-time would cost us dearly. The recruitment of ex-Killie player Mark Roberts in 2009 was not welcomed by some Ayr fans but it did not take long for him to win over the doubters. He is undoubtedly a quality player and in this particular match, a touch of class, as well as great composure, brought Ayr an equaliser with 14 minutes left. Had Roberts snatched at his shot, it would probably have been blocked but instead he controlled the ball, sidestepped a defender and slotted the ball past Craig Nelson to make it 1-1. From the depths of despair, I now believed that we could go on to win the match and when the 'Moff' fired home a left foot drive with two minutes to go, there was bedlam in the stand and also on the park as a mini pitch invasion ensued. Another pitch invasion at the final whistle confirmed Ayr's promotion and as we hugged, jumped up and down and belted out 'Ayr, Ayr, Super Ayr' I was reminded why it is so good to be an 'Honest Man'.

The journey through the stormy weather on the way back home was well worth it. It was as if the weather took a break for the duration of the match and then returned to wreak havoc throughout Scotland overnight. The 100mph winds caused terrible damage in central Scotland and in the area of Tayside we had driven through the previous day. We arrived back in Ayr safely and headed up to Masonhill to Stevie and Karlene's to celebrate our latest victory and to toast our heroes. It was the end of another season, Brian Reid and his squad deservedly won the plaudits for taking Ayr United back up to Division One and the positive mood would surely be the foundation for an altogether more successful season than in 2009-10.

Another Shot at Glory

The summer break from football was the longest I had experienced for some time. My resignation from the Ayrshire Referees Association meant that I would not be officiating at any of the close season youth football tournaments but I was not exactly at a loose end. Another academic year ended in mid-June and I started my holiday break from Ayr College for what promised to be a fun filled summer. My wife's 60th birthday celebrations gave our family and friends a chance to party. We rented The Knowe, a large house in Portpatrick, and 16 of us had a weekend to remember. The following weekend we had a party at home and no sooner had we settled back into our usual routine than the fixtures for the new season were released.

I am never very enthusiastic about friendly matches and so my first game of Ayr United's 2011-12 season was a Ramsdens Cup home tie against Queen of the South. If the straightforward 2-0 win against First Division opposition was anything to go by, we would surely hold our own at the higher level. With the momentum from the combined contribution of 'Somerset Boab', Calvin Ayre and the 'Somerset Ragazzi' added to the feel good factor among the fans, after our successful promotion push, the expectation levels were certainly higher than two years previously. The start of the season saw the team playing a stylish passing game that was good to watch. We even disposed of SPL opposition with a 1-0 defeat of Inverness Caledonian Thistle in the second round of the Scottish Communities League Cup. The wisdom of fielding a weakened team in a Ramsdens Cup match against Annan Athletic however, could be questioned as Ayr lost 1-0 and this result seemed to trigger a lethargic period for the team. Three away defeats, losing four goals in each match, saw Ayr plummet towards the foot of the table and after 10 matches we were rock bottom of the League. The 'boo' brigade was already calling for Brian Reid's head and the big mouths behind me in the Somerset Road end were giving Gareth Wardlaw dog's abuse. In fact, the abuse had started in August, when Ayr played Falkirk at home. With Ayr 1-0 down, the ball landed at the feet of Wardlaw. The clown behind me bellowed out, 'Don't gie it tae that big waste of space'. The words were no sooner out of his mouth than big Gareth slotted the ball home to equalise. I turned round, caught the eye of the loud mouth and shook my head. His response was weak, to say the least, 'It's the first thing he's done aw season,' he protested. It was the third League game of the season. You just can't please some people. Ayr's League results never made pleasant reading but when Hearts visited Somerset Park in late September for the third round of the Scottish Communities League Cup, Brian Reid's team took them to extra-time before dumping them out of the competition, 4-1 on penalties and the scorer of the equaliser on the night was the much criticised Gareth Wardlaw.

Some of the best times I have experienced throughout my years following Ayr United have involved the League Cup competition and here we were, bottom of the First Division but in the quarter-final of the cup competition with yet another SPL team, St Mirren, barring our way to the semi-final. Since the Inverness cup match I had been joking with everyone that our name was on the cup this year. St Mirren had been playing some decent football under ex-Ayr player Danny Lennon's management and beating them at St Mirren Park was going to be a tall order. Tuesday 25 October was yet another one of these terrific nights following the 'Honest Men'. Around 1,200 black and white army recruits made the journey to Paisley, more in hope than expectation. I travelled up by car with Marilyn, Ben and Ben's girlfriend, Gemma. As always, I saw this as another opportunity to add to the Ayr United ranks and when Gemma informed me that she had once been an Ayr United mascot when she was a little girl, I felt confident that, given time, I could talk her into joining our ranks. What better way to start my recruitment drive than a quarter-final win and the anticipation of a subsequent semi-final appearance. We piled into the stadium and after a giant-sized hot dog, with coffee to wash it down, I was ready for another great night of exciting cup football.

To my mind, this match was up there alongside some of the great events in Ayr's history. BBC journalist Chick Young had been singing Ayr's praises, having attended the previous triumphs against Inverness and Hearts but he had predicted that Ayr would finally come unstuck against a free-flowing 'Buddies' team who would apparently be too hot for Ayr to handle. 'There will be no upset tonight,' said Chick. Brian Reid had other ideas and my opinion was that Ayr would need to try and contain St Mirren by defending well and trying to hit them on the break. The Ayr crowd got right behind the team from the start and as always the Ayr players responded magnificently. I never detected any frustration in the away support when it became obvious that Ayr would allow the Saints plenty of possession as they sat deep in their own half. As the 'Ragazzi' banged their drum and chanted their way through the first half, Brian Reid's troops held firm as St Mirren piled on the pressure. I was extremely happy with the 0-0 scoreline after 45 minutes and when I bumped into die-hard Ayr fan Ronnie Johnston at half-time, I was a lot more optimistic than I had been before the kick-off. I reasoned with Ronnie that if Ayr could be more progressive in the second half they could pull off a victory.

The second half went to plan, I suspect, exactly as Brian Reid had planned. Not only did St Mirren fail to find a way past Ayr's resolute central defensive pairing of John Robertson and Chris Smith but United started taking the game to their opponents. The Ayr crowd roared on the team and with eight minutes to go, our stand erupted when Chris Smith rose to head home the winning goal. I was jumping around like a young thing and when I turned around to give my wife a hug; I succeeded only in planting a forearm smash to her face. With no lasting injury sustained, we continued our rendition of 'Ayr, Ayr, Super Ayr,' with the volume turned up. With one arm around Marilyn and the other around Ben, I was in my element. It was another great night to remember. Brian Reid, with the limited resources available to him had now eliminated three SPL teams in the competition and we had made it to the semi-final of the tournament.

We Are Ayr, We're Ayr United

Ayr United, Scottish Communities League Cup semi-finalists. That had a nice ring to it. We would be in the draw along with Falkirk, Celtic and our biggest rivals, Kilmarnock. I relished a match against any of these three teams. Without doubt, the biggest tie would be Ayr United versus Kilmarnock and this match would not only raise the excitement to fever pitch in Ayrshire but it would also capture the imagination of many neutrals throughout Scotland. It was great to have the excitement of a semi-final to look forward to and it was with baited breath I awaited the draw on 1 November 2011 and what a draw it was.

FALKIRK v CELTIC
AYR UNITED v KILMARNOCK

Bring it on, was my first thought. This was going to be the most important Ayrshire derby match, ever. Along with every other Ayr supporter, I would need to wait until the end of January for the one of the biggest matches in the club's history. It was decided that the match would be played at the national stadium, Hampden Park, on 28 January with a 1pm kick-off. The scene was set for another shot at glory.

The anticipation of triumph over our neighbours from East Ayrshire boiled over on New Year's Day. As usual, we were at Stevie and Karlene's in Pine Brae for a party to celebrate the start of a new year. The Killers' *Human* came on and, having had a few beers I decided to change the chorus slightly. Like every other Ayr supporter, the semi-final was never far from my mind and when the opportunity arose I replaced 'Are we human? or are we dancer?' with 'We are Ayr, we're Ayr United'. A few people joined in and the following morning, through my hangover haze, I composed new lyrics for the song and annoyed anyone who would listen to me. I even recorded the new song by singing into the voice recorder on my Christmas present, a new iPhone. The song included the great memory of our famous victory in 1999 and I believed that it would work well as a song from the terracing. It went like this:

(To the tune of the Killers' *Human*)

WE WERE STANDING ON THE TERRACE
URGING AYR TO GIVE US MORE
WHEN THE NET BULGED FOR THE THIRD TIME
ANDY WALKER MADE US ROAR

3-0 TO THE HONEST MEN
WE'RE AYRSHIRE'S NUMBER ONE
CLOSE YOUR EYES, CLEAR YOUR HEART

AND SHOUT IT OUT!

CHORUS

WE ARE AYR, WE'RE AYR UNITED
WE ARE THE BEST TEAM IN THE LAND
AND WE'RE ON OUR WAY, TO GLORY AT HAMPDEN
WE ARE AYR, WE'RE AYR UNITED

REPEAT CHORUS

I may be a sad old man of 57 but my mind is still that of the sycophantic 14-year-old Ayr United fan. I was not in the same league as Somerset Boab but my lyric writing was proving to be therapeutic. I had a new song to practice in the run up to the biggest derby match ever and it was making the wait just a little more tolerable.

After a disappointing start to 2012, with a League defeat at Cappielow, Ayr entered the Scottish Cup at the fourth round stage and it was an away trip to Livingston on 7 January that would put Ayr's excellent cup form to the test. I drove up to the game with Stevie and Andy Smart and we arrived at Almondvale to be greeted with the stadium's fire alarm in full song. After half an hour standing outside in the bitterly cold wind, the fire officers gave the all clear and we finally made our way into the ground to find that it was even colder. Ayr managed to win the match 2-1 to maintain our interest in both cups but the score was a complete travesty. Livingston pounded the Ayr goal for almost all of the 90 minutes but a tap-in from Andy Geggan and a wonder solo goal from Michael McGowan was enough to see the team through to the next round to face Falkirk at Somerset Park.

As one of the biggest matches in Ayr United's history approached, Kilmarnock were making moves to bolster their squad. The acquisition of Ben Gordon, the return of Dean Shiels and a failed attempt to sign Derek Riordan all pointed to a David versus Goliath mismatch on 28 January. That was until Calvin Ayre took a hand to rally all 'Honest Men' with the news that he was prepared to make funds available for Ayr to sign a Scottish Premier League player. With Ryan Stevenson in dispute with his current club, Hearts, there was a possibility that the former player could be returning to Ayr United to line up against our fiercest rivals in our hour of need but alas it never happened. Other candidates doing the rumour rounds of the football forums included Davie Weir from Rangers and former Ibrox goal-getter Kris Boyd. It was turning into fantasy football now but if Ayr never made a signing it was not going to undermine my optimism. This team got us to the semi-final and I had faith in them to take us one step further. I could not imagine any player in the SPL who would volunteer to revert to part-time football with an Ayr team battling to avoid relegation in the coming months. It just was not an attractive proposition. As the days passed, Brian Reid was being openly criticised for not taking advantage of Calvin Ayre's benevolence to bring in a big time player. Meanwhile, the BODOG millionaire was promising to buy Michael Moffat a racehorse if the 'Moff' scored the winner against Kilmarnock. I was getting a little annoyed at Calvin's flippancy. He was turning a serious sporting event into a pantomime.

Seven days to go and a League game against Hamilton at Somerset was our curtain raiser to the main event, while Kilmarnock were entertaining Dunfermline at Rugby Park on the same day. It started so well. In fact, if things had gone as well in the second half of our game as they did in the first it would have been a very welcome three points for Ayr but despite going in at the interval two goals up, Ayr contrived to lose two goals in the first seven minutes of the second period, thanks to appalling errors in defence. Thankfully, the ship was steadied and we managed to hold on for a 2-2 draw. It could have been worse I suppose. I could have been a Kilmarnock supporter watching my team being dismantled 3-0 by Dunfermline, the team at the bottom of the Premier League.

It was a long time coming but when Saturday morning finally arrived we were all up at the crack of dawn, showered, fed, dressed and further adorned with our scarves and hats. After a three-month wait, our big day had arrived. I chose to wear my lucky scarf from the 1970s in the hope that it would bring us the luck that we would undoubtedly need to overcome our Premier League opponents. Me, Marilyn, Ben and Gemma piled into the car at 10am and headed for Glasgow. Ben turned his back on Liverpool for the day to support Ayr United. Quite a sacrifice when one considers that they were playing an FA Cup fourth round tie against Manchester United at Anfield. Stomach churning, I put the foot down once I reached the M77 and it still took four hours to reach the Polmadie turn off on the new stretch of the M74. Well, 35 minutes actually but it seemed a lot longer. We agreed to pick up Madeleine at King's Park train station, as she was staying in Glasgow. The plan was to text Stevie on our arrival in Glasgow so that our crowd could get together ahead of the match. I parked the car outside the station and walked up to the platform to meet Madeleine and as I did, my phone rang. It was Stevie 'Where are you?' he asked. 'I'm at King's Park meeting Madeleine'. 'We're on the train and we're just pulling into King's Park' said Stevie. Sure enough, the train doors opened and Madeleine, Stevie and the rest of our group piled onto the platform. We walked down to join the throng of Ayr supporters in the Beechwood for a pre-match drink and a singsong to whet the appetite for the drama that lay ahead. A quick call to our friends the Bonsors established that they were stuck on the motorway, sandwiched by two Kilmarnock supporters' buses. They eventually caught up with us at the stadium where we negotiated our way through the security measures put in place as a rehearsal for the Olympics. By quarter past 12 we were in our seats and ready for the action.

The Ayr team line-up was not entirely surprising. Brian Reid had opted for a defensive strategy of 4-5-1 with Gareth Wardlaw given the unenviable lone striker role. I had hoped that Adam Dodd, the Blackpool youngster who had impressed against Hamilton a week earlier, would be given a start but he was on the bench. It looked like Ayr would be adopting the same approach as they did in the previous round against St Mirren. Reid would be sending out his troops to defend stoutly and hit Kilmarnock on the break. I approved and I had a nice warm feeling about the outcome, although that could have been the effect of the brandy I had in the pub. When the teams appeared from the tunnel in the South stand, the two sets of supporters competed with their card displays as the roar went up. The Ayr fans broke into 'Ayr, Ayr, Super Ayr,' while the blue and white hordes opted for 'Hello, Hello, We Are The Silly boys'. At least, that's what it sounded like and looking at their cards, the song was appropriate. Why would they have sky blue cards when their colours are Oxford blue?

Ayr were resplendent in their all yellow kit and Kilmarnock, having earlier won the toss and the right to wear their home colours, wore blue and white striped top, blue shorts and white socks.

We were housed in the D1 section of the north stand and I could only describe the mood of the Ayr support as celebratory. As the match started I scanned the Ayr support and it seemed that everyone in our area of the stadium was standing. In contrast, when I looked to my right towards the Kilmarnock support, they had elected to sit in their seats. We stood for the next two hours willing our team to victory but alas it was in vain. For the first 45 minutes of the match, Ayr defended valiantly but it was only in rare moments that they were to be seen in their opponents half. I was still in support of the strategy, especially when the half-time break arrived with the score still at 0-0. If Ayr could come out of their shell in the second half, in the same way as they did in Paisley, it could be our day. Instead, Ayr defended for their lives throughout the second half and we were living on our nerves throughout as wave after wave of Kilmarnock attacks were thwarted by the excellent defending of the Ayr back line, which appeared to number seven at times, and the outstanding goalkeeping of Kevin Cuthbert. After an hour of play, I thought my wishes had come true. Mark Roberts was on the touchline ready to come on as a substitute. 'Get in there Brian, let's take this lot,' I shouted loudly. He was obviously going to push two up front and we were going to give the Kilmarnock defence something to think about. It was about time. The Killie defence had been unperturbed all afternoon but now they were going to be tested. Well, unfortunately Brian Reid never agreed with me. He replaced Wardlaw with Roberts and Ayr continued to defend on their own goal line. It was horrible to watch as a mixture of missed chances and desperate defending saw Ayr to the 90-minute mark, still level. Ironically, Ayr almost scored in a rare appearance in the Kilmarnock half of the field with only a couple of minutes left. If Andy Geggan's curling drive had made it past Cammy Bell in the Kilmarnock goal we may have had a Cup Final to look forward to but it would have been an injustice.

Instead, it was extra-time and now Ayr would need to have a go if they wanted to progress into the Final. That was my view, for what it was worth, but Brian Reid continued with his policy of not losing a goal. I had no confidence in our ability to hold out for another half an hour but when the whistle sounded for the end of the first period of extra-time it began to look like we could perhaps take the game to penalties. It was ugly, it was negative, it was nerve jangling but it might just work. I may have been dissatisfied with the tactics but if Ayr had got to penalties and won the match from the spot kicks, I would have celebrated like it was a great victory for the 'Honest Men'. The Ayr defenders could not quite pull it off and the man-of-the-match, Kevin Cuthbert, was to end up on the losing side, when Shiels and Kilmarnock finally made the breakthrough with 11 minutes remaining. The horrible, sickly feeling I had in my stomach at that moment would last for the next two days as I tried to rationalise my depression. In 45 years of supporting my home town team I have never felt as badly as I did on 28 January 2012. In previous semi-finals and in our 2002 Cup Final I left Hampden Park with a degree of satisfaction and pride at the achievement of my team. On this occasion, I was left with an empty feeling. Unlike the big matches of the past, I had no positive memories of this match. It was all a massive anti-climax. It is important to say that Brian Reid did what he thought was best to get his team into the Final, his players tried as hard as they could and we, the fans, gave the team as much support as we could but collectively, we all lost.

We'll Support You Evermore

I was determined to break out of my depression in time to shout on the 'Honest Men' in their fifth round Scottish Cup tie against Falkirk at Somerset Park. One week after our distressing defeat and we had the opportunity to progress to the quarter-final of the Scottish Cup. The team sitting in second place in the First Division, 16 points ahead of Ayr, would come to Somerset Park, confident that they could progress at our expense but it never quite went to plan for the 'Bairns'. An evening match under the lights bolstered our numbers as Marilyn, Ben, Alan and Andy joined me on the north terrace for the first half. If the first 20 minutes was anything to go by, we were about to be given a lesson in fast movement and slick passing and Falkirk's early reward of a goal came with six minutes on the clock. Our team appeared to be chasing shadows as the team in navy blue enjoyed the bulk of possession but on the 20-minute mark, against the run of play, young Adam Dodd hit a screamer of a shot that came off the underside of the bar and wee Andy Geggan was in the right place to head home the rebound. All was not lost but our group were realistic about our chances in the second half against a young Falkirk team who looked to have too much quality for us to cope with.

The phrase 'football is a funny game' was made for nights like these. God knows we have had our share of dramatic evenings and memorable successes against the odds at our home ground but the turnaround in the fortunes of the 'Honest Men' in that second half was remarkable. Not that there was any luck involved, quite the opposite. Having made our way from the north terrace round behind the goals at the Somerset Road end, we watched enthralled as three times Ayr claims for hand ball in the penalty box were denied by the referee but thankfully there was one that he didn't miss and 'Marko' Roberts made no mistake from the spot. I was happily jumping up and down, hugging Marilyn and joining in with the songs of the Somerset Ragazzi, scarcely believing the transformation of my team. My lucky mascot, Marilyn, was to recover her iconic status after her disappointing performance at Hampden a few weeks earlier. If Ayr had clung on to their lead to qualify for the next round we would all have gone home happy but our team dominated the entire second half, playing some excellent attacking football. I felt that Brian Reid deserved a lot of credit for adapting his second half tactics but at the same time I could not help wondering what might have been if he had adopted this strategy against Kilmarnock in the Communities Cup semi-final. We may have been struggling in the League but this performance gave me back my optimism. If we could replicate this form in the League games ahead of us we would surely climb out of the relegation zone and consolidate our position as a First Division team. Something else we all had to look forward to was a Scottish cup quarter-final against Hibernian at Somerset Park. Bring it on!

Sandwiched between the cup matches against Falkirk on 15 February and Hibernian on 10 March, were six matches that could make or break Ayr United's season. The first of these matches took place in Dingwall against the League leaders and Ayr performed well to bring home a point in a hard earned 1-1 draw with Ross County. Next up was a trip to Firhill with Ben accompanying me on a midweek trip to Glasgow. As we sat waiting for the teams to enter from the far corner of the ground my mind drifted back to 1973 and that epic display from the 'Honest Men', ripping Partick Thistle to shreds with a 5-1 victory to claim a place in the Scottish Cup semi-final, only to be outdone by Rangers' big bruisers and the torrential rain. We were sitting in the very place where the pre-match violence had broken out

39 years earlier as the thugs among the Thistle support showered the Ayr fans with bottles and cans. The 2012 atmosphere was completely different however. A crowd of under 1500 was housed in one side of the ground. Opposite our position, the main stand was completely deserted, as was the enclosure behind the goals and to our right. The grass bank behind the goals to our left, where the intention at one time would have been to complete the redevelopment of the stadium and achieve the 'Jags' all-seated stadium objectives, was testament to the changing fortunes of Scottish football.

A 4-2 defeat sent us back down the M77 with our tails between our legs and more than a little worried about a home match against Livingston on the last Saturday in February. As it turned out, my ever-diminishing confidence was reinstated but not before Livingston took an early lead and proceeded to pull the Ayr defence apart with some slick football. Fortunately, Ayr managed to equalise through the emerging talent of Andy Geggan and against the run of play it may have been but it turned out to be a real turning point in the match with a rampant Ayr United display in the second half to record a 3-1 win that allowed them to leapfrog Queen of the South into ninth place. A point clear of the Dumfries team and a point behind Raith Rovers, with two games in hand to each of them, gave us a fighting chance of surviving in the First Division. The team were looking a lot more threatening than they did earlier in the season but a midweek home match against Ross County ended in a 3-2 defeat. Nevertheless, the spirit shown throughout our team gave me every encouragement for the last three months of the season. With the matches coming thick and fast, as Ayr played their 'games-in-hand', our next task would be to take on the challenge of Falkirk on Saturday 3 March at Somerset Park, a week ahead of our Scottish Cup quarter-final adventure against Hibernian. This was a must-win match for Falkirk if they were to have any chance of eating into Ross County's lead at the top of the table but an excellent team display, topped by a goal from the head of Andy Geggan with 17-minutes left, gave United three more precious points. We were now four points clear of bottom of the League Queen of the South and despite trailing Raith Rovers by one point, Ayr had played one game less. For me it was back to my younger days, impatiently waiting for the next match. A midweek match ahead of the cup quarter-final tie against Hibs saw Ayr build on the good recent form with a 2-1 win at Livingston, so it was an in-form United who would go into the Scottish Cup match daring to believe that we could return to Hampden for an opportunity to lay to rest the ghost of the unsuccessful Kilmarnock semi-final.

Marilyn had negotiated the Saturday off work and we joined 6,000 spectators for a potential shock victory against the SPL team. It was a decent match and the atmosphere added to the occasion but it was a fairly straightforward win for Hibs, by two goals to nil. There was nothing to be disheartened about. Our League form had picked up really well and we had reached a cup semi-final and also a quarter-final. I had a good feeling about our relegation battle and a 2-2 draw against Raith Rovers in Kirkcaldy kept us two points ahead of the Fife team and five points clear of bottom dogs, Queen of the South. What could possibly go wrong?

Well, the following day, Mothering Sunday, our much-loved neighbours, Kilmarnock, had their day in the sunshine at Hampden for the Scottish Communities Cup Final against a high-flying Celtic team who were by then 21 points clear of Glasgow Rangers in a remarkable season in which the famous blue half of the Old Firm had entered administration, resulting in a 10 point deduction for so doing. There was also a distinct possibility that their financial mismanagement could even end in liquidation. There was of course nothing for Ayr fans to worry about. Killie would have no chance against Celtic and it could be an entertaining afternoon, watching our bitter rivals being torn to shreds by the SPL champions-elect. It did not quite work out like that. Kilmarnock kept up their excellent record of not losing a single goal in the competition and their 1-0 victory saw them secure the silverware. Cue another umpteen years of ridicule, torment and condescending remarks from my Kilmarnock-supporting acquaintances. That's life as an 'Honest Man'. I cannot bring myself to begrudge them their glory. All things considered, they deserved their success. The trophy-winning performance of our deadly enemies certainly took the gloss off my weekend but the season was still alive with the prospect of relative glory. At our level that meant escaping the clutches of relegation and we were in with a shout of securing another campaign of First Division football. Nine games left and with tension mounting Ayr United then did what Ayr United do. A home game against Morton ended goalless and it was followed by a 4-1 defeat at Dundee in midweek. The last half dozen games were going to come thick and fast and Ayr's survival in the division meant that they would need to take something from the first of those, an away trip to Dumfries to face bottom club Queen of the South. The table made interesting reading;

TEAM	P	PTS	GD
Ross County	29	62	27
Dundee	29	48	14
Falkirk	29	44	4
Hamilton	29	42	5
Livingston	29	38	-2
Partick Thistle	29	38	8
Morton	29	36	-13
Ayr	29	32	-18
Raith Rovers	29	30	-6
Queen of South	29	26	-19

A win for Ayr would take them nine points clear of Queen of the South and guarantee a play-off spot at worst and with the 'Doonhamers' losing their previous two matches 3-0 and 5-0 I was very confident. Marilyn was off on annual leave from work and we decided to make a day of it.

The last day of March was sunny and mild and we left at 10am driving down, past Dumfries to the Gretna Gateway for a look around the shops before heading back up to Dumfries for lunch. I do not know how we ended up rushing but as match time grew closer we hurriedly took our seats in a pub in the town centre for what turned out to be a quick bite to eat before heading to the ground. It was our misfortune to choose the Queensberry Hotel. We ordered the same meal, steak and ale pie and to be fair the 20-minute wait to be served looked like it would be worth it as the food looked good on the plate. The steak and ale pie turned out to be a hard pastry shell filled with gravy and two or three lumps of something that was passed off as meat. It was truly awful. Actually, when I think about it, it was truly offal. After picking at it for a few seconds we gave up and headed for Palmerston, £16 down and with lost appetites. It could have cost more. We declined the offer of curly fries for £1.40 extra. On the way back to the car a seagull kindly covered Marilyn's jacket with droppings and as I enjoyed the moment she pointed out that it had also managed to catch me. It was not funny anymore. I hate seagulls. We cleaned up as best we could and looked on it as a lucky omen. We could now confidently expect to win the match. As most people know, bad luck comes in threes and Ayr contrived to lose 2-1 to drag the team back into the danger zone at the bottom of the table. The gap between the two clubs was reduced to three points and with Raith Rovers earning a point away to Ross County, with a 95th minute equaliser, they were only a point behind the 'Honest Men'. We were down to the last six games of the season and it was going to be tense. As a veteran of these situations I was not alarmed. Panic stricken, filled with trepidation or maybe worried sick but not alarmed.

At least we were sure of starting the 2012-13 season, even if it was in the Second Division, whereas Glasgow Rangers could be out of business by then. Their financial plight seemed to be worsening and the administrators in charge of the club were by now admitting that it could end in liquidation. The Ibrox giants were at death's door. Ayr United's apparent saviour, David Murray, had deserted us in 1988 to acquire the Ibrox club and he racked up ridiculous debts with his new love in pursuit of SPL domination and European Champions League triumph. After offloading his problems by selling Glasgow Rangers Football Club to the controversial Craig Whyte for £1, it now looked as though it was all going to end in tears instead of the anticipated triumph that he had envisaged for the club 24 years earlier. I am not sure where Murray's allegiance lies now but to me he has proved himself to be nothing but a self-obsessed glory hunter.

The familiar sound of crashing bottles coincided with our next two matches. A 3-1 defeat at home to Partick Thistle was followed by a visit from the new champions of the First Division, Ross County, and their fans had a party at our expense as they brushed us aside with a comprehensive 3-1 scoreline. We were down to the last four games of the season and we were hanging on to our First Division status by the skin of our teeth. The team's form had slumped at this crucial stage and with Raith Rovers now two points ahead of Ayr, and Queen of the South only a point behind, we were looking like strong candidates for the automatic relegation place. There and then I would have accepted a play-off position because it seemed that the confidence had been sucked out of the team. Our team looked disjointed and unsure about what the tactics were. Brian Reid was being given a rough ride by the support and it was looking like he was going to repeat his record of promotion followed by relegation. The roller-coaster ride continued as Ayr went to Livingston and recorded a 1-0 victory to collect another precious three points, a two point gain on our two relegation rivals as they could both only manage a draw.

Three matches left and there was no way I was missing the trip to Hamilton. Some of our away support had dwindled, no doubt convinced that we were fighting a lost cause, but I was fairly optimistic about getting something from the game as I travelled up to New Douglas Park along with Stevie, Andy and another three hundred Ayr supporters. We witnessed a battling display from the 'Honest Men' that unfortunately ended in disappointment and a 3-2 defeat. Meanwhile, Raith Rovers were opening up a three-point gap with a win at Falkirk but on a brighter note Queen of the South lost 4-0 at home to Livingston. It was down to the last two games and it looked like a play-off spot or automatic relegation. A home match against Dundee would be followed by a trip to Falkirk to conclude Ayr United's campaign. The fine line between success and failure was never more apparent. If the team stayed up it would be considered by everyone to have been a good season. However, if it was to be relegation to division two it would be viewed as a disaster. Three points from a 3-2 home win against Dundee, including a wonder goal from Keigan Parker with an incredible bicycle kick volley, secured a place in the play-offs and survival was still in the hands of the 'Honest Men'. Raith Rovers recorded a 3-1 win against Queen of the South on the same day and that result secured the Kirkcaldy team's place in the First Division and sent Queens down into Division Two.

If Ayr were to avoid the same fate as their Dumfries rivals, they would need to negotiate a path to the Play-off Final past Airdrie United in a two-legged semi-final. The first match was at Airdrie on a pleasant Wednesday evening in early May. I had the same song in my head all day, Black Eyed Peas, 'I gotta feeling, ooh, ooh, tonight's gonna be a good night, tonight's gonna be a good, good night.' Me, Ben and Stevie set off for darkest Lanarkshire at quarter to six but by half past six we were back home. A screeching noise accompanied every gear change as I drove up through the Whitletts and Monkton roundabouts and by the time we reached Symington it was obvious to me that the clutch cable could snap at any time. I turned the car and headed back home. We could not very well miss the match so we jumped into Ben's car and headed north once more, arriving in the ground at 7.45pm just as the game kicked off. We should have seen the car problems as an omen. In a one-sided match we were totally outplayed and how we never lost four or five goals is a mystery. A more apt song title for the evening would have been The Eagles *One of these Nights* On a positive note, we escaped with a 0-0 draw and with everything to play for in the return leg at Somerset Park on Saturday 12 May but despite starting brightly the 'Honest Men' had a nightmare match, losing 3-1 and having two players sent off.

So, the curtain had fallen on another season and the depressing reality that we were on our way back to division two was hard to take. No matter how many disappointments I've suffered over 45 years, I've never got used to that sinking feeling in my stomach. Had Brian Reid and his team managed to keep their place in the First Division it would have been considered a successful season. A Scottish Cup quarter-final, a League Cup semi-final and survival in the second tier of Scottish football would have been commendable. However, it was not to be. The team came up short and the relative catastrophe of relegation was the final outcome. For the last match of the season, we stood on the north terrace of Somerset Park, me, Marilyn, Ben, Stevie, Andy and all our football acquaintances as the final whistle of the season ended in agony. The Airdrie supporters to our right danced with one another and goaded the Ayr supporters who had stayed to applaud our team, despite a lacklustre display. Three home team players walked towards our position, applauding the fans in gratitude for their support while, sadly, the rest of the team disappeared into the pavilion with no acknowledgement of the Ayr United fans.

I spent the following day watching the televised last day of English Premier League matches. In the most thrilling finale that I can ever remember, Manchester City took the title at the expense of their illustrious neighbours United, on goal difference. City scored two goals in added on time to beat QPR 3-2 while United's 1-0 win at Sunderland was not enough to stop their rivals. It was stirring stuff but it did not lift my gloom. Maybe tuning into the upcoming Euro 2012 tournament in the Ukraine and Poland would reinvigorate me and bring back my enthusiasm in time for the 2012-13 Second Division campaign.

In the final act of the 2011-12 season, Ayr United manager Brian Reid parted company with the club and I think most 'Honest Men' believed that it was the right time for change. In my opinion Brian did a decent job for Ayr United and I can only wish him all the best in his next venture, whatever that may be. The announcement of Reid's departure coincided with the news that striker Mark Roberts would fill the vacancy as player-manager, so it would be a fresh start in 2012-13. Yes, come August 2012, the 'Honest Men' will be visiting places like Forfar, Brechin and Alloa and I'll be there, shouting on Mark Roberts and the boys in our quest for relative glory.

With 45 years of football experience under my belt, from my four different perspectives, it would appear that success may have eluded me. It is too late now for rich rewards as a player, a coach or a referee. However, as a fan of the 'Honest Men', I remain hopeful that Ayr United will finally win something of note. I can then join with my family, my friends and 15,000 'Honest Men' to celebrate our achievement.

Well, you've got to dream.

Now, I am off to William Hill's to see if I can get a good price for Ayr United to win the Second Division title.